370

NON-FICT

UNDER ORDERS

UNDER ORDERS

The Churches and Public Affairs

BY
ROSWELL P. BARNES

DOUBLEDAY & COMPANY, INC.
GARDEN CITY, NEW YORK, 1961

Permission to quote from the following copyright material is gratefully acknowledged:

"It Could Happen Anywhere but—", from *The Christian Century*, February 2, 1955. Copyright 1955, Christian Century Foundation. Reprinted by permission of *The Christian Century*.

The Return to Japan (Report of the Christian Deputation to Japan). Copyright 1946, Friendship Press. Reprinted by permission of Friendship Press.

An address at the Washington Cathedral, March 1948, by John Foster Dulles. Reprinted by permission of Mrs. John Foster Dulles and the executor of the estate of John Foster Dulles.

"Machine's Mistake Can Doom World," from the New York *Herald Tribune*, January 22, 1958, by Dr. William H. Pickering, Director of the California Institute of Technology Jet Propulsion Laboratory. Reprinted by permission of Dr. William H. Pickering and the New York *Herald Tribune*.

The Annals, September 1957. Reprinted by permission of the American Academy of Political and Social Sciences.

CONTENTS

Foreword

When we consider the position of the United States in the world today the weight of our responsibility is almost staggering.

As a people, we are beginning to be aware of the implications of our national wealth, power, and position of leadership. We take some satisfaction in it. At the same time we are uneasy. The responsibility is burdensome.

We are uneasy also because we are haunted by insecurity. Our military, economic, and technological power is being challenged. We know that an ultimate test of military power would probably bring about our own destruction as well as that of the challenger in an epic holocaust.

Those who are dependent upon us for their security and we ourselves are beginning to realize that the balancing of such powers may no longer be ultimately effective. It is essential, but it is not enough. While we devote most of our energy and attention to technological progress, which is the basis of economic and military power, we know that we cannot in this way solve the fundamental problems of the world or of human existence.

The amazing progress of science and engineering in our generation, which has brought such dramatic improvement in our physical well-being, has not brought us either essential security or happiness. We are as apprehensive about the future as any generation in history, if not more so.

Consequently, people everywhere are beginning to realize that the basic problems of the world lie in the realm of human motives and conduct. Our ability to help the peoples of the world and to maintain our own security is to be determined therefore by moral and spiritual factors. It is these factors that will determine both the effectiveness and the fate of our nation.

These are beyond the capacities of the laboratories and the Pentagon. They are in the realm where the churches claim, and presumably have, competence. But the churches are already burdened with the personal problems of their members and the needs of their neighborhoods. Thus their total responsibility today is almost staggering. It would be staggering indeed if they were dependent upon human resources alone.

At the same time, mutually contradictory condemnations of the churches for the part they play or do not play in the world crisis leave the public confused and many average church members frustrated. On the one hand the churches are accused of intervening in something that is none of their business and for which they have no competence, and on the other they are criticized for not doing enough.

When conferences or negotiations between representatives of governments appear to be futile, some people call for the military leaders to take charge of affairs, while others demand that the churches step in. This does not mean that there is agreement as to what the churches should do. Alarm induces irritation—why don't the churches do something? And yet when the churches do something, many of those who urged them to action criticize their specific actions.

Caught between contradictory pressures, the churches are tempted to do a little in order to avoid the charge that they are irresponsible and yet avoid the charge of unwarranted intervention. Action undertaken under such circumstances is an improvised accommodation to external forces rather than an expression of policy based upon clear principle. It is seldom significant.

The churches actually do have better reasons for what they do than the confused public, including many Christian church members, realize. The confusion that prevails is in considerable measure the fault of the churches for not defining and explaining their role more effectively. They have not done as much or as well as they should have done, but they have done much that has been significant, and they might do much more if they and the public had a clearer understanding of the nature of their influence and the reasons for it.

The purpose of this book is to analyze the role of the churches in public affairs and to give examples of various types of activity by which they exert influence, so that church members and the interested public will better understand the relevance of the churches and help to increase their effectiveness. It has been written in intermittent scraps of time on nights and weekends while serving in an executive post which requires constant attention to a great variety of needs of the world and of people which the churches are being called upon to meet.

It is unfortunate that those who are hard pressed by the demands of each day for prompt and effective action seldom find time and composure to gain perspective for reflective evaluation of their actions. In writing this book, I have taken at least fragments of time to put action under critical examination.

My use of the inclusive term "the churches" refers, in general, to the Eastern Orthodox and Protestant churches—predominantly the latter—which are members of the councils of churches and share in the activities which I analyze. But I believe that Roman Catholics would concur in many points. Sometimes I refer to "our churches" to make the distinction clear.

I plead most earnestly with the reader to remember that I alone am responsible for the views expressed in this book. I am not here writing in an official capacity.

Roswell P. Barnes

UNDER ORDERS

CHAPTER I

Why Are Churches Involved in Public Affairs?

During World War II a rationing board in Washington issued regulations defining the condition under which fuel oil would be available to churches. Those churches that had heating equipment using fuel oil were required, if they could do so, to convert to equipment that would use coal. Otherwise they could obtain oil to heat the church for Sunday morning services but not for weekday activities.

I went to Washington to seek a revision of the regulations. Of the three men I interviewed on the first trip, two said they were church members and sympathetic to its needs. One of them had been an officer of a church in a western town.

Their responsibility was to establish priorities during that period of emergency on the basis of what was regarded by the board as essential to the nation's needs. Consequently, the reasons they gave for the regulations on fuel oil revealed their concept of what a church is and what it does that is of value to the community.

When asked directly what they thought were the functions of the average church, their answer was simple: to conduct Sunday school and public worship on Sunday morning and to baptize, marry, and bury people. Other activities, though perhaps good in moral terms, were not needed in wartimes. Accordingly, they assumed that the church could carry on its essential work if it had heat once a week.

When I showed them letters from other government agencies asking the assistance of the churches with a number of community problems, they were surprised but readily changed the regulations. These problems were of a considerable variety. One was the day care of small children of mothers working in industrial plants. Most churches had kitchens, kindergarten facilities, and competent women to help with this service. Another problem was community moral deterioration, manifested in promiscuity, increasing venereal disease, and absenteeism in industry. The churches were requested to expand their educational and recreational programs, along with a ministry of personal counseling. Thus it was obvious that they had a heavy schedule of responsibility every day in the week.

They had little difficulty in obtaining fuel when the nature of their service was understood. This experience is reported in order to cite the concept which the board members had of the role of the church.

Another case illustrates the same concept. The first regulation issued for the rationing of gasoline to clergymen made provisions only for driving in connection with the conduct of religious services and for critically urgent visitations, as for the administration of "last rites," but not for "social calls."

I soon received a complaint from the ministerial association of a town where the local rationing board had ruled that since only Roman Catholic priests administered "last rites" it was not permissible for Protestant ministers to use gasoline for pastoral visitations. This reflects an interesting concept of the role of the clergy in the minds of members of the local rationing board. The regulations were promptly amended in Washington without hesitation. The pastoral service of clergymen was recognized to be important.

When there was no longer any concern about priorities, a Civil Defense Administration was set up to plan for the organizing of communities in case of disaster—specifically a bombing attack. My offer to assist by convening some church leaders to advise it about the role the churches could play in such an event met with a courteous reply explaining that all community agencies would be treated alike and no consultation was needed.

When a civil defense manual was issued, its only reference to the service of the churches was one item well down the list of committees to be related to mortuaries. A committee of "mature women and clergymen" was to be set up "to bring condolences to the bereaved."

Here was another reflection of a widespread attitude toward the churches. Their reaction was prompt and positive, in some cases indignant. Shortly thereafter the CDA set up a religious advisory committee, called a large national conference of church representatives, and issued a special manual on the churches and civil defense.

I cite these illustrations, not to cast aspersions on public servants in positions of responsibility, but to show one popular "image" of the church according to which it plays no significant part in the life of the community aside from those rites and practices associated with a narrow definition of religion.

It should be noted that in each instance a reasonably satisfactory adjustment was made without controversy or unpleasantness. Other more difficult experiences could be reported.

The men responsible for the original decisions—and for their subsequent modification—were not hostile to the church, nor are most of the people who assume that a church is only a place for religious rites, ceremonies, and instruction. They think it is a good thing to have churches. They would want a clergyman to officiate at weddings and funerals of members of their families. They support the practice of having prayers at political conventions and those of labor unions, the American Legion, and the Rotary Clubs.

Outside Views of a Church

The public actions we have been considering arise from a sympathetic but unexamined outside view of the church. The men involved were in some instances church members, but they were acting in the capacity of public servants representing the interests of the general national community. The law and the public press have a similar perspective.

From that point of view, what is a church? It is one of the voluntary institutions of society, an organized group of people in a community who are interested in religion. A Christian church is one that acknowledges God and professes to serve the cause of Christianity. As such, it is assumed to have some relationship to other Christian churches in the nation and in the world.

All churches, being organized for religious purposes, are recognized by the state as having a right to exist and may be incorporated to hold property and enter into contracts, much as other voluntary agencies that are not organized for the purpose of making financial profit. At the same time, this recognition means that the state assumes responsibility for a measure of supervision.

In some states there are laws prescribing certain requirements with regard to the procedures that must be followed by churches as responsible legal corporations. In New York, for example, the law requires that the polls be open for a specified number of hours in the election of trustees, who administer the real estate and building of a church.

If someone walking on the sidewalk should be injured by a piece of slate falling from the church roof, he could sue the church for damages. As a corporate body it is responsible before the law.

The state seldom interferes in the internal affairs of a church unless it is asked to do so by some party in the church. Disputes about the ownership of a church property or a contract between a minister and a congregation are sometimes brought into civil courts. In such cases the courts usually assume that the laws of the church should regulate its own life. They concern themselves primarily with the question of whether those laws have been observed in the case under dispute.

From the outside point of view of the law, representing the interest of the community as a whole, a church is a corporate institution in society, but an institution with a dual nature: it is in society and yet not of it; it is put under a limited amount of legal supervision by the state in administrative matters but is conceded the right to consider itself accountable only to God and its own discipline in matters of religious faith and practice.

The situation certainly leaves room for ambiguity in the public estimate of what a church is. The more secular the public, the more it is inclined to regard a church as just another voluntary institution existing for the special purpose of maintaining religious rites and practices. As such, it is expected to comply with the prevailing patterns and standards of the community in everything except its own internal life. Therefore, it should not be concerned with other aspects of community life, such as political, economic, or racial affairs, except for such services as justified the rationing board in giving it fuel oil in wartime for a weekday program of community service.

An Inside View of a Church

Let us consider what a church is in terms of its own faith, origin, and history. No one definition of a church in terms of its essential nature and meaning would be acceptable to all readers from the various communions, so I shall not even attempt to give *the* inside view of a church but only some aspects of *an* inside view in comparison with outside views which we have seen.

A church is not a voluntary institution in the sense that other community institutions are. A Christian church has its basic nature predetermined for it. It is the creation of God in Christ. It was founded by Christ. It is not created by its members but only organized by them. Its essential purpose is given to it; it is the Body of Christ and is to carry on His work in the world, to bear witness to Him, to proclaim the Gospel, to help men serve Him and glorify God. Therefore, its essential purpose is not decided by its members; it is only interpreted by them. It is voluntary in the sense that the members make their own choice to respond to this manifestation of God's will rather than to refuse to do so. Every church also has a given authority, the Word of God. No worldly authority may supersede that authority in matters of faith and practice in the life of the church. Most churches also have secondary authorities—creeds, confessions, catechisms, traditions, or consecrated leaders which their members recognize.

This is not an adequate theological definition of a church but only a statement of some of its characteristics for the purpose of indicating that it is under a mandate which is not established by the choice of its members. *It is under orders given to it.* It is the duty of the members to seek to know the will of God. That determines what a church must do; for it is committed to obedience to God rather than to what men, by the standards of human judgment, think is desirable and expedient. Intelligence, under the guidance of the Holy Spirit, is used to understand and interpret God's will for the church.

A Christian church, then, exists to serve God and to witness to His Son Jesus Christ, who is the head of the Church and all true churches, the Lord of the Church and the world, and the Savior of men. What we believe about God and Christ and the Holy Spirit gives us the basis for what a church is and what it must do.

Every member of a Christian church, on the occasion of his confirmation or his being accepted into membership, has made some profession of faith in Jesus Christ. He has at least accepted Christ as God's unique revelation and has committed himself to Him. Membership in His Church is therefore quite a different matter from membership in any other institution in the community.

In still another respect a church is to be distinguished from other agencies. The Church, "the Holy Catholic Church" of the creeds, the universal Church of Christ since its founding, of which every true Christian church is a part and from which it derives its nature, includes people of all nations, races, and classes. These people are all bound together in fellowship by Christ. The mutuality of concern among its members is a part of the nature of a church. "If one member suffers, all suffer together; if one member is honored, all rejoice together" (I Cor. 12:26). This is another characteristic of a true church which it cannot deny, no matter how great the pressure from the community in which it exists as an institution.

What Public Affairs Are

Public affairs include all the interests of the community as a whole and the social forces that impinge upon persons. They are distinguished from private affairs, which are the realm of the individual's conduct by himself, in his own family, or in such voluntary interpersonal relationships with other individuals as do not affect a wider circle of people.

Most social conduct and relationships are public affairs. Even some family matters are subject to public intervention. Marriage is not strictly a private affair. The public interest is indicated in laws with regard to the age of the parties, the persons authorized to perform the ceremony, the registration of the marriage, its dissolution, and the prohibition of polygamy. Some states prohibit the marriage of persons of different races.

A person having a contagious disease is quarantined. The public prescribes limits with regard to the use of private real estate. Sometimes it interferes with what a man does with his own possessions when the community's conscience is outraged, even if no one else is hurt.

Public affairs encompass much more than government and the welfare of the state. They include a great variety of institutions and groups, which are made up of persons. The average citizen is associated, more or less actively, with a variety of organizations—religious, political, social, business, professional, recreational, civic, fraternal, service, and educational. He may be a member of the Baptist Church, the Republican party, the Garden Club, the Chamber of Commerce, the Bar Association, the Grange, the Hunting Club, the American Legion, the Kiwanis Club, the County Historical Society, and the Masons.

Contemporary mass society is conducive to organization. The individual acting alone often seems insignificant and futile, so he associates with others who share his interests in order to satisfy his desire for group experience or to exert a concerted influence. Just as interests often compete with one another, so do the organizations that serve them. This development of corporate groups has been so accelerated in the past several decades that it has been called the "organizational revolution." It is a feature of public affairs.

Public affairs obviously include such matters as the making and administering of laws, traffic control, public education, strikes, the location of industries, gang warfare, television programs, magazines, public parks and recreation, race relations, building codes, celebrations of national holidays, and welfare programs.

Underlying the obvious problems of public affairs are questions about which we have assumptions that largely determine our approach and reaction to the immediate specific conflicts of opinions. We may not consciously have formulated our answers to these questions. We may have unconsciously absorbed the prevailing assumptions of our social environment. Among such questions are these:

What are the major goals and purposes of our nation?

What do we as a nation most fear?

What are the principal characteristics of our culture, of the "American way of life"?

What are the qualities the community most admires in a man?

What contributions of a man to society does it appreciate most highly and reward most generously?

What are the kinds of security that our people seek?

What are the objectives for which people work hardest?

What are the values we most cherish?

Neglect of such questions dealing with the dynamics, the motivations, the evaluation of public affairs leaves us aimless, confused, and—at the deeper levels—demoralized. It is no wonder that we hear of the "lostness" of man, of his loneliness, of the "beat generation," of "angry young men."

Unless we deal with such questions at the deeper levels of public affairs, we shall deal only superficially with such matters as strikes, fixed TV programs, alcoholism, race relations, Christian citizenship, obscene publications, highway accidents, foreign aid, and bonds for public schools. Unless we make a fundamental diagnosis, we shall prescribe only for the symptoms of our ailments. Unless we understand the real conditions of our society, we shall not know what we are talking about when we speak of crises.

There are times in the lives of all of us when events and circumstances crowd in on us with such bewildering pressure that we wonder what is going to happen to us. The tempo and tension of life mount. We call such times crises. Then we think or try to think in broad, comprehensive terms of fate and destiny, not so much of immediate events as of the span of life and ultimate ends.

Similar times come for people in history, bringing with them questions about the fate and destiny of a civilization. We are in such a time now. Our generation is troubled by fateful quandaries.

A Christian as Church Member and Citizen

A church member is not only a church member; he is also a citizen of the nation and community, and as such he shares the outside view of the church as well as the inside view. It is as a citizen that he sues another church member or the church in the civil court. The church is not entirely independent of the civil order, nor is the church member as a citizen free from civil law.

Moreover, civil law is a part of the order of God's creation. It is necessary for the maintenance of order and justice, which contribute to human welfare (Rom. 13:1-7). The individual is under obligation to obey the law unless it is contrary to God's law. It is at the point of the "unless" that the difficult perplexities arise. The fact that the state is subject to the rule of God puts limits on its use of political power. "We must obey God rather than men" (Acts 5:29).

So the church member sometimes experiences tension between what is expected of him as a citizen and what is expected of him as a church member. This may be a distressing tension. He owes his physical security to the state and his spiritual security to Christ and His Church. If the demands of the state conflict with the demands of the church, through which he has committed his supreme allegiance to God in Christ, his conscience is troubled.

In our country the tension arises not so often between the claims of the state and the church as between the member's customary way of life which is supported by community standards and what the church stands for.

People who are members of churches are usually also members of other organizations. Often some of these organizations are for the purpose of serving special interests which may not be consistent with the principles or interests which the church serves. In this situation the individual may find himself in a dilemma. Uncomfortable about taking a position contrary to that of the church, he may adjust himself to the situation in one or more of a variety of ways:

1. He may stand by the teaching or position of the church and seek to bring his associates in the other organization into line with it.

2. He may try to eliminate the tension by denying that the church should take any position on the matter, that it is not the church's legitimate concern.

3. He may try to alleviate the tension by challenging the competence of the church to take a position or by claiming that its position is wrong.

4. He may accept the position of the church but discount its practical relevance to the situation on the ground that it is a good thing for the church to state ideals but that they are for the day when all men will be perfect, or at least for some future generation, not ours.

No matter what position he takes, either the church and public affairs are so far apart that they have no relation to each other, or else they are in tension. Of course, in particular situations, he may be justified in discounting the relevance or the competence of the church, but he will find it difficult to generalize in this way about all positions taken by the church on public affairs. If its position agrees with that of the organizations with which he is associated for the promotion of his own interests, he will probably accept both the appropriateness and the competence of the church's position.

On the other hand, the church member's tension may not be distressing. It may be challenging, because, as a member of the church, he has a sense of mission to express the convictions of his faith in all his community relationships, decisions, and behavior. He knows from his inside understanding of the church that it is much more than just another voluntary community institution. He finds joy in its service.

But whether it is distressing or challenging, the tension is there and he tends to try to reduce or ease it, because life is more comfortable without it. If his daily life in the community as a citizen is comfortable, he doesn't want the church to disturb it. If it is not comfortable, he wants the church to help him make it so, either by giving him comfort in the midst of it or by making the community more comfortable for him.

Thus tension is eased for the member of the church if its influence is on the conservative side, as in some respects it is and should be. Then he modifies the popular outside view of the church and recognizes a wider role for it in the community. He maintains that the church has a social responsibility to provide religious support for what he considers to be the best traditions of our culture.

This is an important role of the church in society. The church has a long history. It sees changes in the perspective of the centuries. Having lived through political revolutions and within many forms of society, change is not too exciting to it. It knows that change for the sake of change is not necessarily good. So it can contribute to orderly continuity.

For the individual, continuity, security and comfort are especially welcome today. Daily life for most people is hectic in its variety of contacts, activities, and experiences. The society in which we live has so many changes coming so rapidly that we need something stable to hold to. So many people move from one home to another so frequently that even the roots that normally work down into a neighborhood, a house, furniture, utensils that have been used in the family for a long time have little to take hold of.

The tempo of history is so fast that we cannot adjust ourselves to a world that is so different from the world of a few years ago. We can hardly imagine what tomorrow's world will be like. This seeming discontinuity of history is one of the major problems of life today. When I was an adolescent, for example, my generation of youth could choose a vocation, prepare for it, and make plans for life on the reasonable assumption that the jobs and professions at that time would still be available for our generation. It is not so easy to plan today. New occupations have emerged. Some of the old occupations have almost entirely disappeared.

Such change is bewildering and frightening. We feel the need for some institutions that do not change or that at least provide orderly continuity and stability. It is no wonder that many people want the church to be such an institution. In a way, it should be and is. It has a conservative role.

It is easy to understand, therefore, why many people are resentful not only when the church itself changes but also when it is a factor in revolutionary change in society. They want it to resist change and to provide a sanction for things as they have been.

We can understand, then, why the older generation in some southern communities, for example, already strained by the rapid change in modern life, feel that the drastic upheaval in their traditional community pattern of segregation is just too much to take. They feel that their way of life is being destroyed, and destroyed by policies, if not principles, which they were trained to believe are fundamentally wrong. Naturally they resent it if the church becomes party to that change.

If these people have been trained by the church itself to think of it as primarily the conservator of social tradition and the source of personal comfort, they can be expected to take the position that it should mind its own business and not get mixed up in desegregation. If it does so, it increases their tension and discomfort.

Another point of tension arising from the difference between the outside and the inside views of the nature and role of the church is the confusion as to what we mean when we ask that a position of the church on a matter of public affairs be "representative." One sometimes assumes that the position of the church should be determined by, or agree with, a public-opinion poll of its members on the matter in question. He may argue that the church should not take a certain position on a matter because a majority of the members he meets on the street, in the club, or in business or professional associations take another position.

He may be quite willing to have the church take the position he advocates and which he reports his acquaintances to take. If he is, he thinks that the church should represent the opinions of its members as expressed in their secular associations.

But a person holding this view fails to consider the factors the church must take into account which may be different, or at least differently weighted, from the factors the chamber of commerce, for instance, considers.

"Blessed are the meek" is hardly a rule of conduct of the market place. "Blessed are the merciful" is appropriately taken into account in a court, but justice is a prior consideration. Yet both of these principles should be in mind clearly in the church.

A group of people may vote one way in a church assembly and another way in the Grange or the Medical Association or the Bankers Association.

The church occasion and environment make a difference. A simple illustration of the influence of the occasion and association is the language people use. Many men and women employ one vocabulary in discussing politics or economics or race with a group of cronies and another in discussing the same matters in the church.

Does this mean that they are hypocrites? The answer is not easy. They are not necessarily insincere. Difficult questions with regard to Christian vocation are raised at this point. The Christian should behave as a Christian in "the world" as well as in the church.

And yet these people recognize that there is inherently and inevitably a tension between the church and the world. It is not altogether to be deplored, therefore, that they use a more restrained vocabulary in the church. Nor is it too surprising when men vote differently on a matter in the church assembly from the way they would vote in an association that exists, at least in part, to serve special interests in society which are their interests. They want the church to speak for their consciences or at least to be the conscience of society.

So when they want the church to be representative of its members, what do they mean by "representative"? Representative of what they think is practically expedient now; or representative of what they think would be right in principle and what they hope will be possible someday?

A characteristic of a church assembly is that it prays for the guidance of the Holy Spirit. It asks for God's light. The members of the assembly cannot enter into that prayer sincerely without an intention to follow the leading God may give them. They believe that the Word of God has relevance to the problems of the world. In the attempt to be faithful followers they may take a position different from that which they take in circumstances where they are more conscious of other interests and other authorities. In the church assembly their judgment is also influenced by the history and tradition of their own church and of the whole Church across the centuries and in other lands. They become aware of what the church has professed under various forms of society. They are reminded, for example, that what they say and do about race problems in the United States affects the witness of the missionaries they support overseas.

The church member is in a difficult position. Assuming that he is a man striving for integrity of character, he does not want to profess one thing on Sunday and another on Monday. He does not want to assent to one principle and live by another.

In this situation he is tempted to relieve the tension either by denying the applicability of the principle to his practical decisions or by trying to rationalize the principle into conformity with his practice while he strives to bring his practice progressively into conformity with the principle to which he assents in his religious faith and in conformity with which he votes in the church assembly.

One of the most baffling frustrations of the preacher in his role as prophet is to have the man in the pew defend him in his exercise of that role as a compensation on the part of the man in the pew for failing to assume a prophetic role himself. This is not without some value, because it recognizes again the tension that there must be between the church and the world if the church is not to be conformed to the world. But it would be much better if both the preacher and the layman accepted their joint responsibility in their respective vocations for an effective and costly Christian witness.

The layman is at the frontier where the church meets the world. It is he primarily who must penetrate the secular order with the Gospel.

The agony of the church, being in the world but not of the world, is at the same time the agony of its members, both clerical and lay. It is the agony of redemption, the agony of the cross which those who follow Christ are called upon to bear. But those who have known the glory of that agony are less tempted to try to be "at ease in Zion" than those who have sought to escape the tension.

One final observation should be made about the member's dilemma:

He should never be admitted to church membership on the basis of an outside view of the church. He should understand the inside view of the church he is joining before he is admitted. It is unfair to him and to the church to join it before he understands what it is. Moreover, the church is inviting division and dissension over a matter that has already been settled for it if it does not make clear to a prospective member the orders which it is bound to obey.

Under Orders

According to the church's understanding of its own nature and mission, it must be involved in public affairs because it must stand for God's work in the world through Christ. It must proclaim to men that He rules, that He loves men and desires men to love Him and to be obedient to Him, that those who love Him must love others whom He loves and for whom Christ died, and that therefore their relation to Him cannot be separated from their relations to their neighbors in public affairs.

The church has no choice but to be concerned with men's personal relations with one another, with what they do as groups, as nations, labor unions, chambers of commerce, patriotic organizations, garden clubs, or political parties. They are still people responsible to God in these groups. The church is also concerned with what the structures and processes of society do to people—government, taxes, education, automation, television, or atomic energy. These affect people.

No aspect of the life of society or the individual's experience is outside or beyond the rule of God and therefore not outside or beyond the concern of the church, which is committed to seek, to interpret, and to do His will.

This may seem to be a startling and exaggerated statement. In immediate experience, religion seems to be a strictly personal and private matter, encompassed within a person's own heart and mind. Acceptance or rejection of Christ seems to be a solitary decision within one's own thoughts and feeling. This is the essence of the privateness of conscience and faith. We who are Protestants emphasize the point that no one stands between us and God. Yet none of us has come to know God without the church and the Bible.

The erroneously extreme individualism of some Protestants allows them to misunderstand some elementary aspects of religious experience by regarding them as strictly private. An unconscious but almost inevitable consequence of this exaggeration is a tendency to think that one's religion can be separated from social relationships and taken out of the context of the church. To one who holds this view, the

business of the church is to induce and assist the individual to undertake to work out his salvation as a matter strictly between himself and God, without regard for his neighbor.

This is impossible according to our faith. In the early Mosaic law, God's commandment that His servants must live in concern for others is clear. "You shall love your neighbor as yourself: I am the Lord" (Lev. 19:18). In answer to the question as to which commandment is the first of all, Jesus answered, "The first is, 'Hear, O Israel: The Lord our God, the Lord is one; and you shall love the Lord your God with all your heart, and with all your soul, and with all your mind, and with all your strength.' The second is this, 'You shall love your neighbor as yourself.' There is no other commandment greater than these" (Mark 12:29–31).

Consistently throughout the Old Testament and the New Testament, God requires each individual to love his neighbors, not only those closely associated with him personally or those congenial to him in kind and interest, but especially those who are weak, those who are in misfortune, those who are not able themselves to obtain what is necessary for their own welfare.

God requires not only a certain attitude and motive in the mind and heart of a person. He requires also compliance with certain moral laws of human relationships. When men disobey or disregard these laws they alienate themselves from God. When a society disobeys or disregards them it has trouble or disaster.

It is clear, then, that the church, which exists to witness to God's revealed purpose, can neither minister to a person as if he could be a faithful servant of God without consideration for his behavior in society nor evade involving itself in the problems of society in public affairs.

Biblical Sources of the Churches' Orders

The major considerations with which we have been dealing are generalizations derived from an increasing consensus among the churches based upon the Bible, tradition, history, and theological analysis. The Bible is our major common authority, so we should review briefly this principal source of our faith.

Bear in mind the question we are considering: Should the churches be involved in public affairs? And the prior questions: What does God require of man in his relations with his neighbor? What does God require of men in their group life as communities and nations?

If we can understand God's will, we shall understand the responsibility of the church. We should not expect to find many specific answers to specific social problems, but we should be able to find guiding principles.

As I started writing this book I reviewed the Bible to see how it shows public affairs to be related to God, how the religious profession of the individual is related to his conduct in the community, what Jesus taught about a man's relation to God and to his neighbor, and what the apostles taught about the conduct of Christians together in the churches.

I made note of eighty-two passages, ranging in length from entire books to single verses. I commend the same exercise to the reader. Even five or ten hours would be rewarding and instructive.

Since my review was conditioned by the questions in my mind, these considerations seemed important:

God rules as sovereign over all the affairs of men—nations as well as individuals.

The children of Israel were called and judged as a people.

The prophets spoke against the social misconduct of the people.

Profession of faith and social conduct were related to each other and to a person's salvation in Jesus' teaching.

Christ is Lord over all creation and history.

To love God and despise one's neighbor is impossible.

The church is a "beloved community."

The church that is "neither cold nor hot" is condemned.

"Fallen, fallen is Babylon the great!"

I suggest that the reader at least review:

The story of the Creation
The Ten Commandments
Judges 2–6; Nehemiah; Isaiah 1, 2, 40, 53; Jeremiah 1, 2, 5; Ezekiel 33;
    Amos
Matthew
Luke 1:46–55; 4:16–19
Acts 4 and 5; 16:16–24; 19:23–41; 26:19 and 20
Romans 8; 11:1–10; 12; 13
I Corinthians 1
II Timothy 3 and 4
Hebrews 2
James 1, 2, 5
I John 4
Revelation 3, 18

This is not a selection of the most important parts of the Bible. It would be much better for the reader to review the entire Bible himself than to be guided by this list. It contains a few rather hasty suggestions to indicate the kind of guidance which should be sought by the Christian in his approach to the theme of this book.

CHAPTER II

Social Problems in the Usual Functions of the Church

The church is involved in the problems of people and the social order in almost everything it does. Whether it likes it or not—and whether it intends to do so or not—it participates in "social action." Even refusal to give attention to a specific community situation influences the forces that impinge upon it.

Public affairs require special actions by the church. But those actions are not likely to be effective unless it is alert to the social implications of all its normal functions. Therefore, before dealing with specific social-problem areas, several roles of the church are reviewed in terms of their general impact upon its members and the community.

Evangelism

The first and basic relation of the church to public affairs is in evangelism. To separate evangelism from the problems of society is to detach it from life.

Evangelism is witness to the good news of God that a man who in humility, penitence, and gratitude accepts Christ and what Christ has done for him is given victory over sin and death. Then God in Christ gives him forgiveness and makes him free.

But to accept Christ is to believe what He said He did by His death on the cross and what God requires of us in our relations with our fellow men.

It is absurd to think that one can accept the last chapter of His life and be indifferent to or reject the rest. His life was a consistent and unified whole, revealing the will and purpose of God for man and for men. Therefore, to accept Christ as Savior is to accept His teachings and way of life as well as His act of redemption at the end. It is folly to try to separate the "social gospel" from the "personal gospel." What He was included what He taught along with what He did.

Evangelism involves bringing men to an acceptance of the sovereignty of God over all of life, the lordship of Christ over the individual, the church, and the world. So, as Christ taught, the great commandment is to love God and neighbor. And the love of neighbor requires devotion to the welfare of all men in their relations with one another— that is, in community, which is the realm of public affairs.

When we speak of humility and penitence we assume the consciousness of sin. The person who thinks he is not involved in sin deludes himself. Every man, when he is honest with himself, knows that sin is too much for him to cope with alone and unaided. Until he comes to the admission and confession of sin, his pride keeps him from accepting Christ.

There were various kinds of sin. The most obvious, and the ones to which most "respectable" people pay most attention, are the sins we commonly associate with immorality. They are the sins of our lower impulses which we sometimes attribute to the natural animal side of our nature. They are often called the sins of the flesh, including the sins associated with sex and the other natural human appetites. They certainly are sins, real sins, and they wreck many lives.

Christ was concerned about these sins. He helped men in their battles with them. But He seems to have been even more concerned about the less obvious and seemingly less dramatic sins—the sins of the spirit: pride, greed, envy, obsession with personal power and prestige, the practice of exploiting other people, eagerness to possess the material symbols of superiority over other people. Cruel gossip can do as much harm as a hot-tempered slap in the face—and it can just as tragically stain the character of the one who does it.

For people who are captives to sin—sins of the flesh or sins of the spirit and distorted values—preaching and pastoral service that interpret to them the meaning of their sins and the judgment, forgiveness, and love of God are aspects of evangelism. The sins in which people are enmeshed may be both private and public matters. The temptations may come from relations with other people in the community and from their own impulses and desires. Their changed lives and conduct influence public affairs. Evangelism, in such cases is an essential part of the churches' responsibility in public affairs.

Analysis of Society

Closely related to the churches' ministry of evangelism—in fact, a part of it—is the analysis of man as a whole: his nature and destiny, the meaning of life, the present in relation to history, history in relation to eternity, the part in relation to the whole, for the whole is not merely the sum of its parts. I do not know you as a person even though I may have the reports of your latest physical examination, your intelligence tests, your family tree, your bank account, your record of education and employment, and your picture. All these data may help me to describe you. But what you really are may not be revealed by a file containing all this information.

The analysis of man as a whole being is especially needed today when most of us give so much of our life and thought to developing specialized knowledge and skills. Expertness in particular aspects of human behavior or of society is useful and important. I would not disparage the contribution of the specialist in one aspect of the problem of men and society.

A magnificent cathedral could not be built without the master stonemason. But his work and that of all the artisans could not create the cathedral without the design and plans for the whole structure conceived and drawn by the architect. The parts created by the artisan have their meaning in relation to the whole. And the work of the architect is only a graphic vision without the contribution of the specialized skills of the artisans.

Understanding Society as a Whole

This matter of broad, comprehensive, inclusive analysis of life is so important that I consider it advisable to use a rather uncommon word to emphasize it. The word is *holism*. I would not build a philosophy around it as some have done, but it is useful to underline my point.

According to the Encyclopaedia Britannica, "Holism (from the Greek *holos*, whole) is the theory which makes the existence of 'wholes' a fundamental feature of the world. . . . It shows whole and parts as aspects of each other; the finite is identified with the infinite, the particular with the universal. 'Wholes' are more than the sum of their parts, and the mechanical putting together of their parts will not produce them or account for their characters and behavior. The so-called parts are in fact not real but largely abstract analytical distinc-

tions, and do not properly or adequately express what has gone to the
making of the thing as a whole."

Individual men and women, and society, need holistic analysis
today to help them understand themselves and make choices and
other decisions.

The social sciences—history especially, sociology, anthropology, psychology, economics, and political science—are useful for the description of conditions and problems. They deal with facts, and it is
essential that we have facts rather than superficial guesses. They deal
with theories regarding limited aspects of behavior. What we need
most, however, is a holistic understanding of the meaning and evaluation of the facts—wisdom in addition to knowledge. A grandmother
with only an elementary school education who has reflected thought-
fully about long experience may be wiser in her estimate of life and
people than her grandson with a degree of Doctor of Philosophy.

Understanding a Person as a Whole

It is important to know *how* people behave, but much more important to know *why* they behave as they do. This is why we need theology
along with all the other sciences, for theology is the science which is
concerned with what man is, his nature and destiny, the meaning of
life and history, God.

The church fails tragically if it only studies and passes on to people
the findings of social sciences along with some moral exhortation and
religious footnotes. Social science books and pamphlets, though useful,
are not sufficient resources for church study groups or for ministers in
the preparation of sermons on race relations, crime, or politics. The
church should provide the most profound holistic analysis and evaluation of society, including but going beyond social science.

A financier whose business collapsed and who attempted suicide
because he had "nothing to live for" knew plenty of economics and
other "practical" facts but did not have an understanding of what his
involvement in the economic order was doing to him. He probably
thought he knew more than the church about economic life and
resented the church's evaluation of it. Perhaps when he heard the
church it was a sermon that dealt with it at the level of economics with
a bit of scolding added, rather than at the level of Christian faith and
principles, going deeper into the economic order than the science of
economics can go. If so, the church failed him. He had been exposed
to the usual church programs of worship, teaching, preaching, and
various activities. He had been exhorted to apply his beliefs in his

daily life but had not been told or helped to discover how to do that, nor had the church analyzed his daily life for him.

People are often subjected to a constant barrage of influences stimulating them to drive and climb for goals the value of which are seldom examined and by means which are seldom evaluated except to determine whether they are within the law. And to keep within the law requires little more character than mere prudential calculation. (This is not to discount the necessity and value of law.) That is not a standard sufficient to make life significant. It is not enough to enable people to understand what makes them free and happy.

People need help to understand the whole man in the whole society in the setting of history. The church, with the revealed will of God, with its ecumenical perspective, with its special responsibility for appraising man and society, values and history, should be foremost in providing that help.

Prophetic Judgment

Much confusion and debate arise in connection with the churches' prophetic role in public affairs. When their activity in this role is disputed, the difficulty usually derives from a misunderstanding of the nature of the church and its mandate. As explained earlier, the church must speak out with a seemingly imperious authority in the name of God, in the light of His law, without fear or favor, by clear and unhesitating testimony. It must proclaim His law as irrevocable.

To do this requires what appears to be courage but is rather, being true to its own nature, trusting in God. The church will not worry about the possible impairment of its "success" as a community institution if it believes it is being obedient to God and is fulfilling its biblical role.

Of course the church is challenged and opposed, perhaps even persecuted. That is no proof of failure except in terms of short-range worldly standards. Popularity is more hazardous for the church than hostility. Jesus said, "Woe unto you, when all men speak well of you, for so their fathers did to the false prophets" (Luke 6:26).

On the other hand, opposition is no sure proof of the prophetic authenticity of any act or word. It is quite possible for one to be irritating for the conscious or unconscious purpose of inviting persecution and seeming to be a martyr. And there are false martyrs just as there are false prophets.

Jesus said, "Blessed are those who are persecuted for rightness' sake, for theirs is the kingdom of heaven" (Matt. 5:10). He did not say that all who are persecuted are blessed regardless of the reason for the persecution. We must be certain that the cause is that of righteousness.

Again, Jesus said, "Blessed are you when men revile you and persecute you and utter all kinds of evil against you falsely on my account. Rejoice and be glad, for your reward is great in heaven, for so men persecuted the prophets who were before you" (Matt. 5:11). He did not say that the frustrated or neurotic person who induces persecution to get attention on his own account is blessed.

It is often difficult to distinguish between faithfulness to God's will and stubborn insistence on having one's own way. On the other hand, it is easy to rationalize disobedience or evasion of responsibility on the ground that we cannot be absolutely sure what God's will is, so we may as well take the safe course and go along with the prevailing way of the world.

When we attempt to discern the churches' responsibility for prophetic judgment, we must use every available resource to discover what is for righteousness' sake and on Christ's account. I suggest ten questions that may help to distinguish the real from the false prophetic witness. They are not all of equal weight, and not all are applicable to every situation. The list should lead the reader to think of others.

1. *What does the Bible teach?* This is the basic question, the starting point for all who profess to believe that the Bible is "the only infallible rule of faith and practice." We should not start with what other authorities say. Bible study is the indispensable ground for all prophetic analysis and witness.

2. *What are the theological principles involved in the matter?* These are derived from the Bible and the thought, life, and experience of the church. Theology is the science on which the church primarily relies. The social sciences, though useful, are secondary. They do not provide the appropriate point of departure for the church's understanding and judgment of man and society.

3. *What do tradition and experience of the church teach?* For centuries the church has been dealing with problems involving the same principles as those to which we subscribe today. It has an accumulated wisdom in addition to what is generally regarded as the revealed truth committed to it and to which it has been and is committed.

4. *How does the matter appear from the ecumenical perspective?* National, cultural, racial, political, economic, and other interests and environments tend to distort analysis and to prejudice evaluation. They may also contribute special insight into a problem. But the church, responsible first to God, should use every resource that helps

it to approximate universal validity in its judgments. The ecumenical perspective is a useful corrective to unintentional partiality.

5. *What does history teach?* The church sees history as the record of human affairs in a universe of which God is the creator and sovereign Lord. Human events have meaning in relation to the law of God. This is different from a secular, mechanistic interpretation of history. Therefore, the church, when it makes a judgment on a particular situation, should review analogous situations in history to find how various human policies have worked out in them. 1140430

6. *Is the church taking a disinterested approach to the matter?* The church should view a situation from the standpoint of what it believes to be God's will and the welfare of all people rather than from concern for the interests of the church as a community institution. When the church is thus disinterested, it will bear witness to the truth as it sees it and not allow its course to be determined by the popular reaction in the community.

7. *Is the church dealing primarily with those aspects of the matter in which it has special competence?* If the church is to provide sound prophetic insight, it should make its own analysis of a situation rather than repeat a secular analysis and add its religious reasons for supporting or opposing it. The church may use facts and judgments from reliable scientific and secular official authorities as part of the data of the situation, but its conclusions should be derived from its own given principles.

8. *Is the church acting as the humble, suffering servant?* Although the church has the duty to speak with firm authority, its authority is derived from its Head, who is the redeemer and suffering servant, humbled on the cross, as well as the judge. The church should therefore never be arrogant, nor should it ever use as a threat any worldly power and influence it may possess. While it should sometimes act in indignation, its indignation should be against affront to God or the well-being of His creatures, and not prideful resentment against insult to its human social prestige.

9. *Is the church "speaking the truth in love"?* The prophetic word is the word from the God of love as well as judgment. "For God so loved the world that he gave his only Son, that whoever believes in him should not perish but have eternal life. For God sent the Son into the world, not to condemn the world, but that the world might be saved through him" (John 3:16–17). So the church that bears Christ's name should bear its prophetic witness out of compassion and with an evangelistic intent to bring men to acceptance of the Gospel.

10. *Has the church earnestly prayed for God's guidance in its wit-*

ness? The church does not rely on unaided human wisdom. It believes in the present power of the Holy Spirit to guide in the interpretation of Scripture and all the other resources for the comprehension of the will of God. It must therefore be constantly in prayer that its prophetic witness may be consonant with God's purpose.

Under such guiding principles, the church that is faithful to its nature and its mandate will make the prophetic witness of judgment in public affairs, serving morality, justice, freedom, order, and peace. It will speak to the groups in control of the power structures of our society. It will evaluate economic and political life, race relations, international affairs, the state, and the nation; for all these are subject to the governance of God.

Education

In order that the church may more appropriately and effectively influence public affairs, it should undertake a much more fundamental educational program both for its own constituency and for the general public. The purpose and substance of such education are suggested by this book. The relatively small space given to it at this point is no indication of its importance, for the whole book is intended to be an educational instrument.

I cannot sufficently emphasize the prime necessity of Bible study. Our own church members are scandalously lacking in knowledge and understanding of the Bible. Consequently, they approach most problems with only a vague idea of the *given* principles that provide the context within which the church and the individual Christian should tackle the problems. They are confused as to what authority is to be taken most seriously. Lacking fixed points of reference, they improvise solutions on the basis of the same factors as are considered by those who profess no religious beliefs.

The Bible study we need will provide us with essential presuppositions in the light of which we must formulate our policies with regard to public affairs:

1. *Elementary theology.* This is a prerequisite. We have made a stupid blunder in thinking that, since theology is a special field of training for the ordained clergy, the lay church member does not need to study it for himself. Unless and until the whole church is more literate in the elements of biblical theology, the laity and the clergy will be in tension. Their minds will not meet, because they approach issues from different "frames of reference"—from different assumptions as to what is most important.

Our education with regard to social problems has been largely on the level of morals and ethics. That is proper and inevitable and will continue to be so. But unless people understand the theological principles from which morals and ethics are derived, the latter will lack basic substance and authority. They will be considered desirable but not imperative, "ideal" but not really essential.

Teaching with regard to Christian morals and ethics is a middle ground ("middle axioms") between theological principles and the concrete, specific problems of life in society. Without an understanding of the principles that provide the reasons and authority—the ground and sanction—for them, morals and ethics tend to become more relative than they should be. They are doubted and challenged by considerations of prudential, pragmatic expedience, and the church is accused of not knowing what it is talking about.

Thus we need Bible study to clarify our understanding of God, His sovereignty, His law and its meaning in history; the nature of man and what determines his destiny; sin—personal and social; the meaning of God's incarnation in Christ; love and redemption; the Cross and resurrection; Christ's teachings about life and man's relation to God and man. This is not a complete list but illustrative of the points at which the Christian's faith determines the morals and ethics by which he must live if he trusts in God.

The teachings of the church with regard to race relations and economic life, for example, should derive from such study. The reader might find it illuminating to list the theological tenets found in the Bible that have a bearing on the problem of racial discrimination. He should think not only of biblical teachings about race but also about God and Christ and man.

2. *The nature of the church.* Enough has already been said in Chapter I to indicate the urgency of education as to what the church is. Most churches give considerable attention to what their own church and denomination do. They give some instruction in the organization and government of the church. But unless we have better education with regard to the essential nature of the church, we shall not be able to understand its role and shall continue to have confusion in the ranks as to its function in the community.

From my observations and experience, it appears that the confusion with regard to what the churches should do about the problem of integration results more from disagreement about the nature of the church than from varying understandings of the Christian ethics of race relations. The churches that don't know what they are don't know what to do.

3. *Other basic factors.* In addition to education in elementary theology and the nature of the church, several other questions should have special attention:

a. What is the relation between accepting Christ as personal Savior and accepting Him as Lord over the church and the world?

b. What is the nature and scope of the authority of science—the social sciences as well as the physical sciences?

c. What are the groups and associations in which pride and self-interest are unconscious or unrecognized? Nation? Race? Patriotic society? Professional association?

d. What are the appropriate and reliable authorities in matters of faith, morals, ethics?

Pastoral Services

So many people have become accustomed to thinking of the ministrations of the church in terms of the services of "the minister" that when they speak of pastoral services they have in mind the services of the ordained clergyman. This is contrary to principle, at least for Protestants. It is not justified by the New Testament record of the early church.

Every professing disciple of Christ, every member of the church, has a pastoral role and responsibility. What is often stated to be a basic Protestant principle—the priesthood of all believers—should more accurately be stated as the *mutual* priesthood of all believers. This latter statement is closer to the position of Lutheran and Calvinistic theology than is the individualistic statement of the priesthood of all believers, which misses the importance of the community of believers and their responsibility to one another in the church.

Pastoral services, therefore, include the mutual helpfulness of all members of the household of faith in Christ's name, both clergy and laity. They also include the Christian service of any member of the church to any one outside the church.

Pastoral services help to bind the members of the church into a fellowship in which each shares the joys and sorrows of the other, and each supports, disciplines, and learns from the other. Thus the person who is lonely in his responsibility and authority in public affairs may be guided and strengthened to live by his faith through the pastoral services, which help to keep him firmly and consciously within the fellowship of those who are committed to God in Christ. It is the fellowship of those who have shared nurture in the faith and in the discipline, forgiveness, and inspiration of the sacraments.

Thus, also, every member who is caught in the loneliness of the depersonalized mass forces of society is supported by the fellowship. Pastoral services help him to feel that he *belongs*, whether he gives or receives those services. He is influenced most by the associations that mean most to him. If in his participation in public affairs he is influenced more by the bar association, labor union, or the like than by the church, he probably feels that he belongs to it more intimately than to the church. One of these groups may have provided him with a substitute for the pastoral services he should have been giving and receiving in the church.

If other associations have more effective authority over him than the church has, it is probably because he has deeper emotional dependence upon them than upon the church. And it is the pastoral relationships among fellow Christians in the church, at least as much as its teaching authority, that give him the security he needs and influences his conduct and decisions.

The Mutual Priesthood of Believers

It should be emphasized that giving is fully as essential as receiving. When a member is giving, he has the sense of being needed. This is as important for his feeling of belonging as is his gratitude for what he receives. The *mutual* priesthood of believers in pastoral service is of the essence of the fellowship of a Protestant church. The Roman Catholic doctrine of the priesthood of the clergy provides a cohesiveness in that church around dependence upon the authority of the priest. We Protestants have what we believe to be a doctrine closer to the nature of the church of the New Testament, and more effective. It provides cohesiveness around the mutual priesthood of the believers, the fellowship of the members of the churches. But if we fail to practice our belief, we have less upon which to depend, having repudiated the theory of the unique and superior priesthood of the clergy.

The development of pastoral services in the fellowship of the church is therefore important for the influence of the church upon its members in their daily life and consequently through them upon public affairs. This constitutes an especially difficult problem for the big church in which the members hardly know each other. In the small church it is not so difficult, because it is more natural and obvious for the members to be personally helpful to each other.

During World War II many churches, especially in Europe, were left without ordained ministers. Some almost fell apart. But others carried on as fellowships of believers supporting one another in pastoral service, relying on the ordained clergy only for the functions of administering sacraments and for giving theological instruction. Some even undertook serious biblical and theological study, using the libraries of their absent pastors. Such experience contributed to the renewal of the spiritual vitality of many churches and to their increased impact on public affairs, both through their individual members and corporately as churches.

Much may be learned about public affairs through pastoral relationships. A certain minister was criticized by members of the congregation for preaching about housing, unemployment, public health services, and community recreational facilities. He was accused of talking economics and politics, about which he had no special knowledge. He realized that the people who took exception did not know what he was talking about—what he had on his mind.

He asked some of them to help in specific ways in homes where help was needed. They responded willingly, assisting where crises had arisen because of illness, domestic problems, and the like. In volunteering, they became interested in the families and their difficulties and in the process acquired a sympathetic understanding of the problems they found. Gradually housing, unemployment, public health services, and community recreational facilities came to be regarded as problems of human beings. Economics and politics were involved, to be sure; but the church members, by becoming involved in simple pastoral services, began to understand why the minister preached about such matters. Criticism and tension subsided. The whole church became deeply involved in public affairs, even to the point of making specific recommendations to the city council and appearing at hearings.

The Minister's Counseling

Having underlined the significance of the mutual pastoral services of the lay members of the church, we turn to the pastoral services of the ordained minister, for he has a special role by reason of his ordination, training, experience, and his full-time employment in the work of the church.

One of his first responsibilities is to lead the members of the church into pastoral services for the sake of the people and of the church. And he cannot lead unless he himself has an intimate knowledge of the actual lives of the people. Moreover, the insights he gains in such relationships are highly important for his evangelistic, prophetic, and teaching ministries. His work is rather superficial and irrelevant if he does not know the situations of the people with whom he is trying to communicate.

The wise and conscientious minister knows not only the usual behavior problems of the church members, but also the fears and ambitions that drive people to disaster or to high achievement. Such knowledge is essential to preaching and to pastoral counseling. It requires a basic understanding of public affairs, of the dynamics that prevail in society as a whole and in the groups in which people participate.

Consider, for example, the relation between pre-marital counseling and public affairs. Without much assistance many young couples can get fairly well acquainted with each other's habits and tastes, likes and dislikes, during courtship. But they often find it difficult to talk to each other about the values they believe to be most important in life for them. Being in love, they cannot be expected to be objective. They try to be honest with each other and they probably are, but they need help.

Many young men, for example, misjudge their fiancées with regard to income. If a couple discusses the matter seriously, the girl will probably say—and mean it—that she will be content with whatever he can make without "killing" himself, or with whatever they can make together and still "have some life together" and have a family. He will probably think she is very loyal and reasonable but that the more money he makes the happier she will be.

After marriage a young husband may drive himself, work nights and weekends, join groups that may help him get ahead—all because he thinks his wife wants it. She, however, may think that he is more interested in his work and his outside associations than in her and their home and family, and she may secretly resent what he is doing because she misunderstands. But she will not reveal her thoughts because she does not want to interfere with his life.

In this case the pervasive popular standards of success and happiness so victimize fine but immature young people that they find it difficult to be themselves with each other. They need pastoral counseling to help them arrive at basic mutual understanding from the beginning, before they get caught by social pressures. The consequences of this kind of agreement on values and on other considerations of what will constitute life fulfillment for them are very far-reaching. Such agreement influences—perhaps determines—their choice of groups with which they will affiliate, the extent to which they will support groups to fight for their own economic advantage. It determines in large measure whether they will become involved in politics as a public service or as a means of achieving power—in fact, whether they will be politically responsible in any sense.

Thus pastoral counseling in values and life objectives, whether giving assistance in immediate interpersonal relations or in any other situation, is directly related to the contending forces in public affairs.

Reconciliation

The church, by any valid definition of its nature and function, has a concern for the welfare of the whole community and for every sector of it, whether the community be a local neighborhood, a nation, or the world. The church is commissioned to help all, whether "saints" or "sinners," and to proclaim the Gospel to every creature.

Where there is tension—antagonism or open conflict—between individuals, groups, or nations, the church should be an influence for reconciliation. Since it includes—in principle at least, and often actually—people who are set against each other in public affairs, it should be able to serve as a bridge for communication, mutual understanding, and the resolution of destructive controversy.

This is all quite obvious and apparently simple. But it is not simple. Many churches are unable to render an effective service of reconciliation where it is most needed. This is because these churches lack certain essential qualifications.

A church must be scrupulously fair if it is to be helpful in a conflict. It must carefully examine facts and reports without prejudice. It must neither assume that the underdog is always right nor that power, either that of majority opinion or of effective influence, is always right. It should have courage to describe a situation as it sees it, regardless of popular reaction. It should demonstrate that it is "not for sale," that it is not influenced by fear or desire for favor.

However, to be fair is not necessarily to be morally neutral. This point needs emphasis and clarification, because some people who value very highly the reconciling ministry of the church do not want it to "take sides" lest it impair its usefulness.

The church dare not be neutral in the sense of being indifferent to truth and justice, content to assist in the negotiation of a compromise of positions for the sake of peace.

If contending groups are to accept the church in a reconciling role, they must have firm confidence that the church is so completely dedicated to truth and justice that it will recognize and accept them wherever it finds them, even though it may have indicated an inclination to support one of the parties to the controversy. Fundamental and undeviating commitment to truth and justice is fairness. This is why fairness is indispensable in the church that attempts to fulfill its ministry of reconciliation.

Notice that I spoke of *moral* neutrality. There is a sense in which neutrality is essential—that is, neutrality as to which party will seem to gain advantage—for the objective of the church should be not that one party prevail over the other but that truth and justice prevail.

Unless both parties are prepared to rely on truth and justice, they will probably shy away from the church. Unless the church can be trusted to stand for truth and justice, it does not merit the confidence of either party.

I have been referring to reconciliation that deals with two parties together. But there is another process of reconciliation where the parties do not meet because of the unwillingness of one or both. Then each must be interpreted to the other. Here again the church, whether or not it assumes that one side has a better case than the other, must be interested not in which side seems to win but in truth and justice.

To be helpful in reconciliation, it is necessary that the church have an understanding of the predicament, the hopes and fears and loyalties of the people with whom it is dealing. It cannot be helpful to people unless it knows them. This means that the church must include within its fellowship members from the sectors of society that are in tension. When the owning and managerial group compose the constituency of one church and the labor group compose the constituency of another church in the same community, neither church can be very helpful in a strike situation. The two together can accomplish something.

Good will is essential, but without knowledge and understanding it is futile. Of course perfect understanding is not achievable. It is presumptuous for any person or group to claim that it has arrived at complete identification with another. However, long and close associa- tion in Christian fellowship in the life and work of the church provides the basis for a large measure of understanding. This is one reason that political tensions, which can be quite acute, seldom split churches in which there are members of the rival parties in considerable numbers.

In the ministry of reconciliation a church may act as a corporate body, asking different sides to explain their positions, issuing analyses and appeals. It may demonstrate in its own fellowship how people holding contrary positions can discuss them and associate together in good will. It may exert its influence through its lay members, or it may either support its minister in such work or at least not object when he undertakes it. Whatever form of expression the ministry may take, the qualifications and disciplines mentioned are essential. This observation applies to rendering assistance in building understanding in interpersonal relations as well as in economic and industrial life, politics, race relations, social caste resentments and fears, and international affairs.

Demonstration by Example

Numerous well-chosen adages emphasize the relationship between what we do and what we profess to believe. "Actions speak louder than words" and "What you are speaks so loud I can't hear what you say" are among the most familiar. These are often applied to the church by those who try to discredit it and also by some who are willing to take its witness seriously but hesitate because of what seems to them to be insincerity.

The church professes to be committed to manifesting God's will in the world. It is assumed to be in some sense the custodian of the Gospel. Its own life is constantly under close scrutiny by both the skeptical and the hopeful. Therefore, what it is exerts an influence in public affairs along with what it teaches and preaches.

A caution must be inserted here against concluding that the church should not bear witness to the Gospel in preaching and pronouncement until its own house is in order. The Gospel, as God's Word, has its own authority regardless of the behavior of the church. It is not dependent upon validation by the church's practice. We cannot wait to condemn race discrimination until we have eliminated it completely in the churches. We should not wait until our country is consistently Christian before sending the Gospel to other peoples who have not heard it. We should not refrain from telling the good news of God to our neighbors until we think we are worthy disciples. We are commanded to preach the Gospel which has come to us.

Even so, the church should strive persistently to bring its own life into conformity with what it professes. If in its own fellowship it transcends the racial, economic, and class cleavages of the community, it can help to heal them by example. Any church that does not give a welcome to all people is handicapped in its witness to the community as a whole. A church should not act as if it were a private club belonging to one group or sector of the community.

Even if a church does not refuse admission to anyone or "freeze" him out, it may by its conduct and spirit make it obvious that it is under the effective influence or control of certain elements, or that it is unduly influenced by prevailing worldly standards.

When a church boasts about the important people it has among its members and officers, it indicates what kind of reputation it wants. It implies quite clearly that it seeks a prestige derived from the community's standards of popularity. To be true to its nature, the church should choose as its own leaders the most outstanding Christians, on the basis of their character and insight. They are not always the bankers, managers, merchants, lawyers, or others prominent in public life.

One church which was careful about its choice of leaders included among its elders the senior partner of a famous law firm, an apartment-house doorman, a wealthy real estate operator, a cabinetmaker, a doctor, an investment broker, and a public-school teacher. They were chosen because of the depth of their commitment to Christ, their loyalty to the church, their mature faith, their upright conduct, and their sound judgment. Anyone, no matter what his station in life, could feel at ease in that church. The community knew that within the councils of that church were people who understood the problems of all sorts and conditions of men and were interested in them.

The attention which the minister gives to people is another indication of the church's concept of its role. Favoritism is inexcusable, whether the members demand it or not, but many churches take it for granted. This was made clear to me early in my ministry. As a member of a committee of clergymen, I had undertaken an assignment which I had not completed when the committee met. I offered the excuse that I had conducted three funerals in two days, all of which had taken considerable time because of long trips to cemeteries. One of the older men advised me that I should not take time to go to the cemetery myself "unless it was somebody important." Who, I asked, is important? Anyone who is in distress in the presence of death should be regarded by the church and its minister as important.

The church either confirms or corrects popular standards of value in human life by its own demonstration of whom and what it considers to be important.

It can also help to develop the Christian qualities of community by encouraging mutual assistance among its members. This is seen in rural life when the church rallies its members for a barn-raising or for equipping a house for a family that has been burned out of its home.

Some churches assist their members in organizing credit unions, which are groups of "persons associated together for the purpose of building up a fund with their own savings and of making short-term loans from this fund, at reasonable interest rates, to members of the groups" (*The Church and Credit Unions,* by Benson Y. Landis, National

Council of Churches.) Of some, 244 credit unions organized among
members of local churches in the United States and Canada, 963 were
in Roman Catholic Parishes and 250 within Protestant churches as of
1956.

Weddings and Funerals

Weddings and funerals provide various opportunities for influencing contemporary society. Some so-called wedding managers and
some funeral directors take over the church and use it as an auxiliary.
The result is an occasion that becomes predominantly secular, sometimes almost pagan. Families sometimes encourage or even insist upon
the superior role of such people. It is the responsibility of the church
to assert its authority and refuse to be relegated to an obsequious
secondary status. When it yields, it sometimes finds itself in a position
where it is even difficult to maintain proper decorum. When it permits
lavishness and extravagance on such occasions, it fails the people
directly involved and also the community. (Of course there are funeral
directors and wedding managers who co-operate in maintaining appropriate standards for these occasions.)

These are, in a sense, public affairs. But in their essential meaning
they are still generally recognized to be religious. The church cannot
expect to have an influence in other public affairs that are assumed
to be secular if it surrenders control of these that are more obviously
its own domain.

Economic Practices

Employment policies and personnel practices with regard to wages
and hours should be watched carefully by churches and their agencies.
These matters are sometimes so complicated that we tend to improvise
arrangements that will "get the job done" without considering whether
what we do is appropriate or just. We cannot here examine the problems in detail. A few questions will suggest the factors that should be
considered.

Should a church entice a minister from another church by offering
him a higher salary? Should a minister leave a field that needs him and
go to another that needs him less but can pay a higher salary and thus
enable him to provide a better education for his children? Should a
minister be dependent to any considerable extent on funeral or wedding fees? Should he accept such fees?

One actual incident will illustrate the implications of such questions for the role and influence of the church. The best man at a wedding handed the minister an envelope, explaining that it was his fee. The minister declined to take it, saying he did not accept a fee for a religious service to anyone connected with the church. The best man was so surprised that he blurted out an inappropriate expletive and then in red-faced embarrassment apologized profusely for his language and said, "I never knew a minister who didn't take all he could get!"

The excited best man was impressed. Subsequently he called the minister for an appointment. Eventually he was received into the church on confession of faith. He became quite a missionary among young businessmen, telling them that the church is not just another institution building up its own prosperity.

We should be cautioned not to make an unjust comparison of the minister in the illustration with all ministers who accept fees. In this case most of the credit should go to the members of the church, who advanced the salary of the minister by an amount estimated to match the income previously derived from fees.

Should churches raise money by games of chance—bingo, lotteries, or selling guesses on the weight of a cake at a church bazaar? The question is not so much one of the moral issue of petty gambling—though that is not irrelevant—as of what it does to the concept of the nature of the church when it appeals to mixed motives and uses trivial devices for obtaining its support.

Mutual aid among churches may be impressive testimony to those outside its ranks. When German Lutheran missionaries in Indonesia and elsewhere, shut off from their normal source of income during World War II, were supported by our churches of other denominations, the meaning of Christian solidarity was demonstrated convincingly.

Community Service

Churches are related to public affairs through the welfare and educational services they provide. Hospitals, schools and colleges, settlement houses, homes for the aging, recreational centers, summer camps—all these make an impact on the people they help. They are also part of the community pattern. As such, they involve relationships with other agencies, tax-supported and private.

Through their agencies the churches may gain insight into conditions and needs in somewhat the same way that individual church members do through pastoral services. In fact, such agencies may be pastoral-service extensions of the church.

Probably much more important than the service of such agencies is that of the churches themselves. It is unfortunately necessary to make this a qualified statement by saying *probably*, for some churches become ingrown, concerning themselves only with serving their own members and their families, having no sense of responsibility for the people around them or for the community as such.

I remember vividly a conference in an exclusive club with a committee from a church which was looking for a minister. The committee had heard me preach, had made some inquiries about me, and were apparently interested when they invited me to lunch. They gave me a proud account of the history of the church, the important people in its membership, the beautiful sanctuary, modern parish house and educational building, excellent music, ample parsonage, large salary, staff assistance, long vacation, allowance for travel abroad to gather interesting material for preaching—just about everything they thought a minister could want. Then they asked me some reasonable but not too probing questions about myself and family. They were perfect gentlemen, interested in their church and devoted to it.

Next they invited me to ask them questions. Feeling somehow uneasy about the glowing account they had given me, I asked about their program. It was good. They seemed quite satisfied with what they had. So I asked at what points they thought the work should be improved or expanded.

This question apparently took them by surprise. For a few moments they tried out some tentative ideas on each other. One of them mentioned a new housing development which had recently been completed a couple of miles from the church and to which they had given little attention. But the others observed promptly that these people probably would not feel at home in this church. They wouldn't fit in well. The church was such a congenial fellowship that it would be a mistake to bring in this new element.

They were perplexed and a little troubled when I told them that I did not trust myself to go into such a comfortable church and that I would be more interested if they had some problems on which they wanted help or some ambitions for more effective or expanded service. I explained that I was disappointed by their attitude toward the people in the new small houses.

I believe I may have failed those men and that church. In a way, they were the church. On the other hand, either the church had developed in them the standards and the concepts of the church which they reflected to me, or the secular world had given them those standards and concepts and the church had failed to challenge and correct them; so they were not to be blamed any more than the church.

Fortunately there are not many churches like the one described, but there are enough to make it necessary to say that *probably* more important than the community service of the churches' welfare and educational agencies is the service of the churches themselves. The normal church—normal in the sense that it is typical of the prevailing standard and practice—has a sense of responsibility to the people around it, to the nation, and to the world. It takes pride in what it does as a corporate body of Christians in the total life of the community.

A list of the services of one particular church suggests what may be regarded as normal:

1. Surveying conditions and needs in the community.
2. Studying the programs of the community agencies.
3. Co-operating with other community agencies.
4. Recruiting volunteers to serve in other agencies.
5. Supporting and participating actively in the work of the council of churches in its service to the wider community.
6. Organizing and supporting its own standing committee on community relations.
7. Co-operating with the police in locating and anticipating trouble and correcting situations that encourage delinquency and crime.
8. Sharing in the sponsorship and leadership of community events.
9. Making periodic door-to-door canvasses to extend a welcome to the church to those who are not affiliated with any church.
10. Providing a forum where candidates for public office may state their position and face questioning.
11. Drawing children, youth, and adults from the neighborhood into the educational, social, and recreational program of the church.
12. Providing Big Brothers or Big Sisters for adolescents who have been before juvenile courts.
13. Organizing and providing facilities and leadership for Camp Fire Girls, Girl Scouts, and Boy Scouts.
14. Befriending and sponsoring foreign students and refugees.
15. Collecting used clothing for Church World Service and World Council of Churches for use overseas, keeping a limited stock for local needs.

This same church has made a practice of including in the reports to its annual congregational meeting a list of its members who serve on committees or give other voluntary assistance to such agencies as the YMCA, Salvation Army, settlement houses, hospitals, and youth boards. Some from that list are included in the membership of the standing committee on community relations.

All such activities should be closely co-ordinated with the pastoral and reconciling ministries of the church. In fact, they may be regarded as aspects of those ministries when they are kept close to the heart of the church's life.

Statements and Resolutions

The role of the churches in formulating, adopting, and issuing statements and resolutions should be considered in the light of our understanding of the nature of the church and of public affairs, the mandate of the churches—biblical, theological, and historical—the competence of the churches and their responsibility for evangelism, holistic analysis, prophetic judgment, education, pastoral service, reconciliation, and community service.

Because of the public attention given to statements and resolutions, some people seem to think that they represent the churches' primary contribution to, and involvement in, public affairs. Such people are found not only among those outside the churches but also among those who are members but are not active in or concerned with the many other activities of the churches in connection with social problems. As a matter of fact, statements and resolutions are a relatively minor factor in the churches' total influence in public affairs.

However, even though relatively minor, they are highly important. The process of formulating them focuses the educational procedure within the churches on concrete situations. It reminds the churches that they cannot be content with never-ending and indefinite discussion of general ideas while decisions are being made and issues determined. If the churches are to be relevant to history, they must seek to influence it. An inconclusive review of various positions may help to put prevailing confusion into a pattern, but any secular analyst can do that. The churches are under obligation to appraise in the light of Christian principles.

As we saw in Chapter I, when Christians consider carefully and seriously the bearing of their faith on a problem of public affairs or human relations, they usually find that the reasoning based on practical popular expediency is not the same as that which is based on the Bible or on theology. It makes a big difference what our starting point is. If we have already taken a position on the basis of secular arguments and then think about our obligation to take Christian principles into consideration, we tend inevitably to seek justification for the conclusions we have already reached. We try to find scriptural quotations or theological authorities to support us. This is to "use" the Bible and religion, as the devil can quote scripture for his own purposes.

But when we start from the presupposition that religious truth is elementary, that the Bible is our rule of faith and practice, we see contemporary problems in a different perspective, and secular authorities have less weight.

Prayer and Bible study are much more than "devotional exercises" for cultivation of the "spiritual life." They are essential to orient us and our lives to God and to commitment to His will. They help us to be attentive to the Holy Spirit. If we try, consciously or unconsciously, to use them to prove ourselves right in a conclusion at which we have already arrived, we try to make them instruments of our own pride. Prayer and Bible study for the purpose of learning what God would say to us is quite a different thing from prayer and Bible study for the purpose of finding strength and support for what we have already decided we think and want to do.

In prayer and Bible study we see all of life under God's law. We see people as His children for whom Christ died. We take the long view of history and realize that what seems to succeed for the moment may not endure. Values fall into a different order of priority from the rating of the secular world, mercy and deeds of compassion becoming more important, and economic, political, and social rank and power less important. We become humble before the redeeming love of the Cross. We have faith in life over death, the spirit over the flesh. We are reminded of the lordship of Christ over the Church and the world.

In a fellowship thus enlightened, disciplined, and inspired, we view the problems of the world from a perspective quite different from that which influences the analysis and conclusion of most of the groups with which we are associated in our political, economic, and social life. It is from this perspective that the church must speak in the world by statements and resolutions.

The formulation of a statement requires first an analysis and evaluation of the social situation in the light of our fundamental beliefs, then a focusing of the principles inherent in these beliefs upon the particular social problem in the setting of the social situation.

By approaching the problem in this way, the church should provide a more profound, valid, and helpful understanding of it than any other authority can. It should be the church that gives people their deepest insights into race relations, the rights and responsibilities of organized labor and capital, the limitation of armaments, immigration policies, and legalized gambling.

The church must speak also to bear witness in the world. (See

Prophetic Judgment, above.) Impelled by its concern for contributing to a solution or amelioration of the problem, the church must not only deepen understanding in terms of principle but must also investigate and study the facts. It cannot analyze the problem without knowing the facts, and it may be alert to and discover relevant facts that specialized experts in social science overlook or discount. The mayor's committee may provide an impressive set of facts about the increased revenue which might be available to New York City from taxes on legalized off-track betting, but there are also other facts with regard to what gambling does to public and private morals which the committee neglected.

Getting the facts about a problem also includes learning about the interests, motives, and reliability of the groups and authorities that are taking sides on the problem and trying to influence the public.

Thus the process of preparing, discussing, and revising statements is educational and informative in analyzing the situations which affect the daily lives of men, women, and children and the concrete problems to which our Christian faith must be applied if it is to be relevant.

A statement not only serves as the church's witness; it also enables individual Christians to articulate their convictions. Those members of the church who have not participated in the process of preparing the statement are reminded of the tension between the church and its values and the world and its values. Some of them, being comfortably adjusted to the world and its values, either by conviction or by gradual and unconscious rationalization, or an accommodation of their faith, resent being put into tension between the church and the world. It is a tragic fact that many of them have been nurtured in the church in a very incomplete understanding of the Gospel. Therefore, the church itself shares in the responsibility for their confusion and distress. Moreover, some of them may have been offended at some time by a statement made by the church more to demonstrate its courage than to contribute to an understanding and solution of a problem.

Obviously the church should not allow threats of any kind to deter it from bearing its witness. Withdrawals of membership or financial support, condemnation by governmental or private groups, a split in the ranks—these and other measures of attack should not intimidate a church. The church especially must resist promptly and decisively any encroachment upon its freedom. On the other hand, such opposition should be met with quiet, firm dignity lest irritability impair both insight and spirit, and action be devised and approved for the purpose of "teaching a lesson" to those who attempt to frighten it into silence.

So we see again how important are the point of departure and the consequent purpose out of which a statement is formulated. The church must be faithful to what it believes to be the will of God and not be guided by what it thinks will be popular. When people formulate and vote upon church statements, they should bear in mind the nature of the church and its role in society, especially its prophetic responsibility. Otherwise they will try to bring the church into subservience to their own or their social group's special interests.

It is sometimes argued that the church should not make a statement about a problem until and unless it has brought its own practice with regard to the problem into conformity with what it would state to be the will of God. For example, some object to the church's condemnation of segregration in public education or other public services as long as segregation is to be found at any point in its own life. To be sure, the witness to professed belief is much more effective if it is supported by practice. Consequently, confession of failure, along with self-judgment, is a part of prophetic witness. But the church cannot wait until it is perfect before bearing testimony to what it believes to be God's will for the church and the world, any more than the individual can wait to be an evangelist until he himself is completely obedient otherwise.

Prayer

We have become so obsessed with the place of power in human affairs—scientific, nuclear, political, economic power—that we act as if it were the only effective factor in history. We have learned so much about how to influence, if not to manipulate, people's choices and decisions by mass psychological impacts and how to help them with their fears and tensions by psychoanalysis that we often neglect prayer.

It is necessary, therefore, to suggest here some of the points where prayer is a very important aspect of the church's relation to public affairs.

I have already emphasized the necessity of prayer and Bible study to provide the starting point for the church's understanding of God's will. The church prays for itself in that aspect of its nature in which it is a human institution, conditioned by history and subject to human error. As such, it prays for humility, confessing its faults and failures. It prays for understanding, for strength and courage, for help to be faithful to God and Christ. It seeks the guidance of the Holy Spirit in the interpretation of the Word of God.

The church should intercede for leaders in public life in all positions of authority and responsibility that God will give them wisdom, teach them humility and obedience, and strengthen them to bear their burdens well. Such prayers should be not only for professing Christians and our own leaders but also for all whose decisions affect the lives of the people anywhere, including communist rulers who deny God.

There are many millions of people carrying burdens of trouble, perplexity, and temptation. For them also we should pray. Consider, for example, how many Negroes in our country are torn between love and hate, good will and violence. One of them, a taxi driver in Washington, said to me, "Pray for me not to lose my faith and get nasty." He meant it.

At a luncheon of a church group in a New York hotel, the "blessing" before the meal included thanks to God not only for the food but also for the labor of many who had brought it to us. At the close of the meeting one of the waiters said that he had noticed the prayer and that it was the first time his work had been "noticed in a religious way."

I expressed surprise and have thought often about what he said next: "You know, there'd be a lot less fighting and a lot better work if people knew they were being prayed about." Fighting is usually a public affair, a symptom of a social problem.

Both the people who ask a minister to pray at a large public occasion and the minister who does so share the responsibility to bring the crowd to silent attention, if possible to an attitude of reverence, before proceeding to prayer. To have prayer in the midst of distraction, confusion, indifference, and disdainful inattention may contribute to contempt rather than respect for God and the church. Prayer should never be permitted to be exploited to obtain a coloration of conventional moral respectability. Public occasions usually provide the minister and other earnest Christians an opportunity to do some education and to bear a witness in their relations with others as well as to salute the sovereign Lord and seek His blessing.

We should not forget the importance of prayer with reference to the problems and temptations of special groups of people. In one church in New Jersey, laymen pray in the church service for others in their own line of work—a lawyer for lawyers, a skilled worker for skilled workers, a doctor for doctors. Such prayers are likely to be deeply understanding.

No special argument is needed to convince Christians of the urgency of prayer in relation to public affairs, and it is hardly appropriate to suggest special techniques and procedures. The sensitive and responsible Christian has two cautions constantly in mind; first, to beware of carelessness and thoughtlessness; and second, not to pray for God's support of "our cause," but to pray that His will may be done and that we may understand it and be obedient to it.

CHAPTER III

Relations with Other Agencies

The churches' involvement in public affairs inevitably brings them into association, directly or indirectly, with a great variety of organized groups. They cannot act in complete isolation.

Such association involves difficult problems of policy. This chapter suggests some considerations to be borne in mind in relation to government, voluntary citizens' groups, and other faiths. It is a further development of the role of the churches.

Government

Once when several of us were taking our leave of the President after a conference with him at the White House, he invited us with more than casual courtesy to come again. He would welcome us, he said, because we did not come to plead some narrow special interest of our own but to talk about principles and the general welfare. Many of his visitors came for the purpose of pressing requests for the benefit of individuals or groups, pleading special interests or advising him on partisan strategies.

What is true of that President's experience is also true of many leaders in government, from the President to the mayor of a small town. Most of the influences brought to bear upon them are exerted by those who have axes to grind.

This point has implications for the role of the churches in relation to government. It suggests that representatives of the churches should call on a government leader sometimes when they have no other purpose than to remind him of the prayers and concern of the churches for him as he carries his burden of responsibility.

It suggests also that the churches should usually make proposals of policy within a broad framework of the basic needs of all the people. This is not only a matter of good strategy; it is also appropriate to the nature of the church. If other religious groups have made overtures which we believe we must challenge, we should not do so in terms of our own prerogatives or in order that our own views should prevail, but should state our case in terms of principle.

If the outcome seems to indicate that our presentation may have had some effect, we should give credit to the official for wisdom and should make no public claim to credit for ourselves to enhance our own standing. We should take satisfaction that what we consider to be the right thing has been done.

There are times when we find it necessary to support values and traditions in our national heritage that are threatened. The practice of other countries may be cited against us, as in the frequent proposals for a national lottery. In such situations we should present our case for what we believe to be right, supported by our own history, and not insist that we Protestants should have our way just because we have been the major influence in American tradition. We contend for the moral welfare of the nation.

Sectarian Considerations

Contacts by our churches with public officials should be made only on a basis which we would recognize as appropriate for other religious groups. We would be offended, and properly so, if Roman Catholic Church officials had secret lines of communication and influence in centers of authority in government. We should not do what we would not want them to do. (I am not speaking of confidential pastoral relationships.)

In one situation I considered it necessary that the President be approached on an important issue of national policy in such a way as to avoid publicity in the press, which would have been unavoidable if a regular appointment had been listed on his schedule. In a certain respect it would be a secret conference. It involved a matter in which there was a general difference in policy and objective between Protestants and Roman Catholics. There was certain information about the matter which the President did not possess.

I knew a Roman Catholic through whom an off-the-record conference with the President could be arranged. He had close association with leaders of his church. Under the circumstances, assuming the knowledge of what was taking place could be made known discreetly and appropriately to Roman Catholic leaders, I considered it appropriate to arrange for a conference that would not be general public knowledge.

The Roman Catholic through whom the appointment was arranged knew the general purpose and substance of the conference. Not a word was spoken about his keeping this information to himself. The important consideration was that certain information be communicated to the President lest he make a decision in ignorance. Even so, secret communication would have been inappropriate—that is, keeping the fact of the communication secret from another interested group which is a significant part of the American community.

Whether or not the ecclesiastical leadership of the Roman Catholic Church knew what happened, I do not know. I never sought to discover. What is important is that there was not a secret line of communication and influence from Protestants through Protestants to a center of authority in government.

This is an illustration of the principle that one religious group should not have a pattern of relationship with government which it would not concede as appropriate for another religious group.

Self-Respect and Good Manners

Another negative caution arises from the fact that since the church represents—in principle at least—the highest interests of society it is sometimes assumed that it is justified in seeking its own institutional purposes by almost any means. The ends are so obviously good that the means are presumably justified. For example, churches sometimes support measures to legalize games of chance that provide financial profit for a church but prohibit such games in social clubs.

Sometimes churches are discourteous and threatening in dealing with government, disregarding the ordinary requirements of good manners. Such practices bring both the church and religion into disrepute among the ethically sensitive.

The attitude with which the church approaches government reveals the church's concept of itself. It is the servant of God and man. It is also—when it is true to its calling—the prophetic instrument of God's judgment and mercy. Therefore, when it approaches officers of government it should be neither arrogant nor obsequious.

When a designated representative of a church speaks to a person bearing responsibility, he should speak with firmness, confidence, and with respect, and at the same time with a sense of the dignity of the church. He should not hold the person in authority in the secular power in contempt, nor should he try to ingratiate himself because of the person's public prestige or power.

Occasionally it is the responsibility of the church to remind leaders of government that the state is not morally autonomous but that it subsists under the governance of God; that church and state together are trustees of a national heritage that rests upon religious grounds and sanctions; and that God gives light and strength to those who are obedient to His will and put their trust in Him.

Where the Church Has Special Competence

There is one area of public policy in which the interest of the church and religion and the interest of society are so closely tied together that the church should appropriately defend its own interests. That is the area of religious liberty.

If the liberty of the church is impaired, religious liberty and all other liberties are jeopardized. In this case, a church should not seek any liberty for itself which it does not seek also for other churches.

In their relations with government, the churches should speak within the scope of their competence, their information, and insights. This is not to say that they do not have practical and specific knowledge with regard to public problems. On the contrary, they often have sound and useful counsel derived from their experience, study, and knowledge in operating their own programs of service.

A missionary who has spent a life of disinterested service in some other country may know more about the habits, impulses, and desires of the people than government officials who may have had only academic training and limited experience in formal negotiation or administration.

The churches, which have resettled many thousands of refugees in this country since 1948, know more about them than do any other agencies, including government. They testify on the basis of superior competence when they appear before congressional committees on legislative proposals concerning the procedures for taking care of refugees. On the other hand, they have no special knowledge about the influence of refugees on the labor market and the general economy of the nation. They may, because of their interest, become well informed on such matters, but their information is secondhand.

With regard to general immigration policy, the churches probably have a competence at least equal to that of any other community agency; for moral, ethical, and historical factors are important if not basic. And the churches are concerned with the total welfare of the nation and the immigrants.

Thus, in connection with national policy, the churches have expert competence at some practical points, substantial but secondary at others. Obviously, when they approach government on this matter, they speak with authority on some issues and only tentatively and with deference to superior knowledge on others.

On some questions of social policy, churches involved in social welfare services through their own institutions or parishes have considerable knowledge and insight. Through their pastoral relations to families and individuals they acquire knowledge about problems which is superior to that of the indifferent citizen and most community agencies. Such knowledge is useful to government at the local, state, and national levels.

The Church Representative's Status

When representing a church body, the spokesman should have credentials indicating the capacity in which he acts and documentation of the position he states. He should be able to state clearly not only the position but also the basis of the church's concern and the nature of its competence.

When the spokesman goes beyond the statement he has been authorized to present, he should make it clear that he is speaking only for himself. This is necessary, especially if he is pressed to interpret the intent of the statement which he has conveyed to a congressional committee. He should ask the committee to distinguish the official statement from his own comments.

Although there is no standard outline for a church statement addressed to government that would apply to all instances, the following points may be suggestive:

Identification and description of the group making the statement
Occasion and date when the statement was adopted
Competence of the church
Grounds on which the church takes its stand—biblical, theological, historical, moral, ethical
Statement of the position
Record of the vote—explanation or statement of minority dissent (if any)
Authorization for use of the statement

Pastoral Service to Leaders in Government

In addition to the contribution which the church makes to the understanding of a problem of public policy, and perhaps even more important, is the pastoral relationship to the person carrying responsibility in any branch of government.

This relationship, to be helpful, should be close enough and sensitive enough to provide an understanding of the perplexities, quandaries, and temptations of the vocation of government service.

Decision is often agonizing for a public leader. The keener the sense of responsibility, the more difficult the choice between courses which are seldom clearly good or clearly evil. Decisions that are obvious are easy; they are hardly decisions. When trusted friends give conflicting advice, decision is hard. When the choice seems morally clear but unpopular, the question arises as to how far one should compromise with his principles in order to keep the voters in line for the next election.

For people working under such tensions, sympathetic moral support is a great help in the struggle to maintain integrity. And moral integrity must undergird social wisdom and political skill in the useful public servant.

Therefore, if the pastoral ministry of the church to such a person is to be effective, it must be based upon a sufficiently close association of the pastor with the problems of the public office so that he will be aware of the time of crisis and the moral aspects of the crisis. Then a timely reminder of the supporting, encompassing fellowship of the church is most helpful: a two-minute visit before or after a crisis, or even a telephone call; a special handwritten prayer left on his desk; a scriptural or other sentence delivered unobtrusively—something not calling for any reply. The pastor need not comment on the substance of the issue but only remind the person facing crisis that God's help is available to him and that he is upheld by the prayers of the church.

Few people are aware of the personal loneliness of many a public leader. The greater his responsibility, the keener his isolation. There is no one to make his decisions for him. His subordinates are inclined to tell him what they think he wants to hear. His rivals do not speak on the basis of impartial judgment.

Unfortunately, if he has power and prestige, even the church is tempted to play up to him and seek to absorb stature from him. When it yields to this temptation, it fails him, demeans itself, and brings contempt upon the church generally. It fails him especially, because it

yields to one of his most insidious temptations—ambition for power—
and thus deprives him of the help he knows he most needs.

This analysis of some aspects of the relation of the church to government has dealt both with government in its corporate and institutional
operation and with people in positions of government responsibility.
Both should be kept in mind. The role of the church as analyzed here
is, I believe, consistent with our national policy of separation of church
and state (see Chapter V).

Other Community Agencies

The church is in a sense a community agency. However, as we have
seen, it is much more than that. It is a different kind of agency. Should
it, then, take its place along with secular organizations in a general
community council or in a special alliance to support or oppose a
particular cause or measure? Or should it stand by itself because of its
unique nature?

In an important sense, the church is involved in every situation in
which its members are involved. It exerts an influence through the
agencies in which its members participate. Some argue, therefore, that
the church as an institution, as a corporate group, need not and should
not be listed along with trade unions, business organizations, wom-
en's groups, and service clubs. Others maintain that the church as
such should show where it stands and exert its corporate influence.

Obviously it makes a difference what the purpose of the association
with other agencies is. Consider first the more general and permanent
organizations. Most will agree that the church or its appropriate agency
should be a member of a social welfare council or a joint non-partisan
committee for civic betterment. On the other hand, few would expect
it to be a member of a chamber of commerce or a labor-union council.
But there would be a difference of opinion on whether it should be a
member of a council against race discrimination in housing or of a
committee for civil rights legislation.

Where there is such a difference of opinion it is especially important
to understand the nature of the community organization before making a decision on whether or not the church should be affiliated with
it. If it is a "clearinghouse" for exchange of information and the voluntary co-ordination of the actions of its several members, a church can
participate without being committed to any policy or measure in any
way against its will. Such an organization has no authority to act on
behalf of its members. It does not itself take positions, at least not without the specific authorization of each of its members.

If, however, it is a "united-front" organization authorized to act on behalf of its members, the church cannot participate without running the risk of being committed without its consent to a position or action or way of doing things which it cannot approve. A majority vote of member agencies, which is the usual rule for secular groups, cannot be accepted by the church, which has its own standards.

Therefore, even when the general purpose of the organization is one which the church may appropriately support—as in the example of opposition to discrimination in housing or promotion of civil rights legislation—the church should be free to make its own decisions on the specific measures to be supported and the way in which they should be supported. For this reason the church is usually better off in a clearinghouse conference than in a united-front organization.

Moreover, if in a particular situation the church desires to support the position of a united-front organization, it can always do so in its own way, stating its own reasons. In some instances the church can be more effective acting independently than the united-front organization with a dozen member agencies.

In its relations with other community agencies the church should guard itself against both aloofness and being "used" by other groups. Even the well-meaning may not understand the church, and their lack of understanding may be the result of the church's staying too much by itself.

Whether or not it officially participates with other agencies in common organizations, the church should find ways of bearing its witness among those who share some of its social and ethical concerns. It should not hesitate to use reliable resources of information and specialized skills developed by them.

The church should also welcome opportunities to discuss public affairs with other community agencies in order to bring the insights of the Christian faith to bear upon the problems and the people. Frequently we find our friends in the secular agencies eager to listen to our analysis of the theological roots of the problem. They are often perplexed and frustrated in their work. The most confused and insecure may be the most dogmatic and intolerant in their manner and statements. If we do not try to embarrass them or beat them down but rather seek to give a deeper analysis of the problem, we may win their respect for the church and assist them in progress toward deeper understanding and even faith.

Our Roman Catholic friends are often more ready than we to work with community agencies, and they are articulate with regard to the nature and the grounds of their concern. They are not afraid of being contaminated by secular associations. I wonder sometimes whether Protestants are shy of such associations because of insecurity at the point of fundamental theological analysis.

The Minister and the Layman

We have been considering the role of the church as an institution in the community in relation to other community agencies. But what of the minister? Is his role that of a representative of the church or that of a Christian citizen? When the Rev. Mr. Brown, minister of the Methodist Church, is a member of the Committee for Interracial Understanding, is the Methodist Church more involved in the committee than it would be if Mr. Smith, a layman in that church, were a member?

These questions reveal confusion. Our prevailing assumptions are not consistent with our principles. We Protestants do not believe that the clergy are the church, yet we expect the minister to have a stricter deportment than that of the average member. We regard him as the symbolic representative of the church when he becomes involved in public affairs, yet we repudiate him if we disagree with the position he takes. When we want to disavow him, we say that he is acting as a private citizen; yet if he claims to be acting as a private citizen, we insist that it is impossible for him to act as such when he is minister of the church.

This confusion is not entirely unfortunate, for it arises in part from a recognition that every member is a representative of his church, and in part from a realization that the minister, by his professional vocation and training, presumably has at least a theological competence above that of the average member.

The extent to which the minister is assumed to represent his church when he works with community agencies varies somewhat according to denominations. Generally speaking, the more the church magnifies the priestly function of the minister, the more he is regarded as the symbol of the church. It is easier for a Baptist minister to assume the role of a private Christian citizen than for an Episcopalian clergyman to do so. So it is impossible to state clearly how much a church is related to community agencies when its minister is related to them. Certainly it is assumed that it is related more obviously through the participation of its minister than through the participation of an average lay member. But in either case the church as such is not represented fully except by a delegated person specifically authorized by action of the church.

Whether the minister is commissioned by his church or takes the step on his own initiative, he has a special responsibility to represent the Christian insights and disciplines bearing on the cause or proposal under consideration.

If he spends considerable time working with other community groups, he should not be criticized for neglecting his pastoral responsibilities. If he is doing such work as it should be done, he is providing a pastoral, teaching, and evangelistic service which is a part of the mission of the church.

Similarly, a layman doing the same thing as a fulfillment of his Christian vocation should not be accused of neglecting his service to the church, for an essential part of his service to the church is to participate in its mission. The man who spends an evening representing his church on a community recreation council is as much engaged in the work of the church as the man who spends an evening at a meeting of the board of trustees. The woman who represents her church on the interagency committee for hospitality to foreign students may be serving the Kingdom of God as much as her friend who is an officer of the missionary society.

Whatever the pattern, an important contribution of the church in public affairs is its association with other community agencies which share some of its social purposes.

Relations with Specifically Christian Agencies

Special note should be taken of the relation of the churches to community agencies which are Christian in title, tradition, and purpose; specifically, the Salvation Army, the Young Men's Christian Association, and the Young Women's Christian Association. They serve some of the same purposes as the churches serve in Christian witness and social welfare. They are allies of the churches.

The Salvation Army has some of the characteristics of a church. It is a member of some councils of churches. But it has a special kind of organization and discipline. It emphasizes certain types of ministry and develops corresponding specialized competences. It is a close ally in certain types of evangelism, youth work, and social service. In some community councils it renders the same Christian witness as the churches.

Because the Salvation Army, the YMCA, and the YWCA are members of the United Service Organization, the churches themselves have not considered it necessary to affiliate with that agency in its work among men and women in uniform.

The YMCA and the YWCA, as independent, voluntary lay organizations, may be regarded as auxiliary or supplementary to the churches in the general pattern of community organizational relationships. They do not presume to take the place of the churches. They may appropriately participate in some associations with secular agencies when ecclesiastical agencies would regard their own participation as questionable.

The relationship between the churches and the YMCA and the YWCA varies from country to country and community to community. In some places it is very close, in others remote. In the same place, one Association may be closer to the churches than the other. There should be mutual understanding of the reasons for the differences, whether they derive from history, deliberate policy, or indifference on one side or the other.

Other Faiths

Roman Catholic churches and Jewish synagogues and temples are to be regarded along with our churches as community agencies concerned with public affairs. We here consider our relations with them in civic life rather than in matters of faith, religious observances, and corporate religious practices.

Problems of differences in religion may arise in connection with association in community interests, for social policy is often so closely related to religious belief that debate on theological difference may arise quite unexpectedly.

For this reason some community agencies prefer not to include representatives of churches and synagogues. They fear being distracted if not disrupted by religious controversy. Some groups which recognize the importance of religion and religious institutions invite a Protestant minister, a Roman Catholic priest, and a rabbi to attend their meetings in rotation so that there will be less risk of religious argument.

There seems to be less fear of non-ecclesiastical agencies. However, complications sometimes arise from the fact or the assumption that Roman Catholic sectarian agencies are often more under ecclesiastical influence or control than are the Protestant and Jewish agencies.

The more co-operation by religious institutions in public affairs, the better for the community and for the general interests of religion, provided it is authentic and not based on compromise. To achieve such co-operation, there should be an understanding that co-operation in public affairs does not imply indifference or neutrality in matters of religious beliefs. To have this understanding explicitly stated from time to time relieves the conscientious representative of any of the faiths of the necessity to define his approach to each problem and thereby induce varying statements by the others.

It is much better for the churches and synagogues to be represented by convinced and loyal believers in their respective faiths than by people who take the position that it makes little difference what a person believes so long as he is sincere and genial.

Easy and Difficult Areas of Co-operation

It is easier to achieve co-operation among religious institutions on some public problems than on others, because on some there are only secondary sectarian differences of interest or approach, while on others the differences are so pronounced as to be major factors in the problems themselves. Although the list would vary according to local situations and leaders, it may be helpful to call attention to some illustrations of matters on which effective co-operation has been achieved among national agencies and some on which it is better not to assume the possibility of official public co-operation. Among the matters on which sectarian groups usually have sufficient common concern to make public co-operation possible are the following:

1. Justice and good will in racial and cultural relations
2. Peace and many aspects of international affairs
3. Humanitarian service to refugees
4. High standards of chaplaincy service in the armed forces and in public hospitals and prisons
5. Justice, peace, and order in industrial relations
6. Fair practices in political campaigns
7. High standards of integrity in government
8. Constructive measures to deal with juvenile delinquency
9. Social welfare in general
10. Opposition to materialistic secularism, notably as expressed in atheistic communism

Among the public problems on which there are substantial differences of policy, approach, or belief, making public co-operation frequently difficult, are the following:

1. Legalized gambling, lotteries, and bingo
2. Public policy and legislation with regard to birth control
3. Tax support of sectarian educational and welfare agencies
4. The general pattern of church-state relations

   5. Religious instruction and observance in public schools
   6. Sabbath observance
   7. Regulation of traffic in alcoholic beverages
   8. The basic problem of Arab refugees
   9. Censorship or organized boycotts of allegedly immoral books or entertainment
  10. The role of government in the regulation of moral conduct

Reducing Contentiousness

We should not jump to the conclusion that there is no possibility of mutual understanding on this second list of problems. Not all Jews or Roman Catholics or Protestants agree on any of these questions, so it is not justifiable to assume that we know what our neighbor thinks about these matters merely because we know his religious affiliation.

At the same time, it is a mistake not to recognize some generalized differences in the positions prevailing among the different religious groups. We should try to understand the reasons for those differences. Through discussion with other groups we may be confirmed in our commitment to our own position, or we may find some common ground on which we can stand together.

We may discover that we have not been careful to explain the reasons for our actions, and that when we make clear what our purposes are some opposition will disappear.

After discussion, differences will undoubtedly persist; but there is a probability that contentiousness may be reduced and the issues joined at a higher level.

Even though there are deep-rooted differences among religious groups with regard to the regulation of the sale of alcoholic beverages, sufficient agreement is found concerning the problem of drinking drivers to make possible the co-operation of such groups with other interested agencies, governmental and private. The National Safety Council has been supported by Roman Catholics at least as much as by Protestants in its effort to reduce drinking by drivers.

When there is uncertainty whether co-operation of religious groups is possible in connection with a matter of community policy, it is advisable to make private informal inquiries before issuing formal public proposals, in order to achieve as much mutual understanding as possible.

CHAPTER IV

Christian Unity and International Conflict

The very rapid growth of Christian unity in our time has enabled the churches to make new contributions to the alleviation of some of the most crucial problems of public affairs, especially the tension between nations and races. The relationships among the churches of the world increasingly demonstrate how the whole family of God is to live if men are obedient to His law.

Christian unity is not in a fundamental sense created by men. It is a gift of God in Christ. Men acknowledge it, bear witness to it, and strive to live in accordance with its requirements when they are obedient to God's will.

Not all professing Christians accept these implications of their faith, and no Christian lives in full conformity to God's law. There is still much hostility among those who have taken the name of Christ. Even so, the churches generally live together in a pattern and spirit of relationships which are quite different from those which prevailed a generation ago.

The principal manifestation of this development is the World Council of Churches, which was organized at Amsterdam in 1948. It is a visible demonstration of unity by 172 national denominations in more than 50 countries, which acknowledge "Jesus Christ as God and Savior" and consider it important to manifest that essential unity despite their secondary differences. In this common commitment they seek constantly to reduce the areas of division and to eliminate contentiousness in the disagreements that persist. Mutual understanding has been vastly increased.

Space permits only a brief review of the prior developments that made the World Council possible: co-operation among missionary bodies, largely through the International Missionary Council founded at Edinburgh in 1910; study and conferences on the beliefs of the various churches concerning the nature of the church and its basic doctrines, fostered by the Faith and Order Movement; co-operation in matters of common concern in the interest of human welfare, promoted by the Universal Christian Council for Life and Work; cultivation of better international relations, in which the World Alliance for International Friendship through the Churches was an important factor; and the influence of ecumenical Christian agencies more or less closely related to the churches but not controlled by them, including the YMCA, the YWCA, the World Student Christian Federation, the United Bible Societies, and the World Sunday School Association.

For the purposes of this book I report certain events indicating the relations among the churches shortly before, during, and after World War II. War is the greatest problem of public affairs. National loyalties are most demanding and extreme during a war period, thus presenting the crucial test of Christian unity.

Oxford, 1937

International tensions had become critical with the rise of Mussolini in Italy and the consolidation of Hitler's power in Germany. Nationalism threatened to disrupt the fellowship of Christians and at the same time emphasized the need for strengthening that fellowship across the lines of antagonism.

Thus the threats to Christian unity and the deterioration of the international situation combined to produce a sense of urgency with regard to the conference of the Universal Christian Council for Life and Work, which met at Oxford, England, in 1937. Its theme was "Church, Community, and State."

Dr. J. H. Oldham, chairman of the International Research Commission, defined the purpose of the conference and the whole accelerated program of co-operative study among the churches as an attempt "to understand the true nature of the vital conflict between the Christian faith and the secular and pagan tendencies of our time, and to see more clearly the responsibilities of the Church in relation to the struggle."

Participants did not think that he exaggerated the crisis in writing: "The Christian foundations of western civilization have in some places been swept away and are everywhere being undermined. The struggle today concerns those common assumptions regarding the meaning of life without which, in some form, no society can cohere. These vast issues are focused in the relation of the Church to the State and to the community, because the non-Christian forces of today are tending more and more to find embodiment in an all-powerful state, committed to a particular philosophy of life and seeking to organize the whole of life in accordance with a particular doctrine of the end of man's existence, and an all-embracing community life which claims to be at once the source and the goal of all human activities; a State, that is to say, which aims at being also a Church."

The standing and competence of the conference are indicated by the authors of the papers in the preparatory volume, *The Universal Church and the World of Nations*, among whom were the Marquess of Lothian, English parliamentary and colonial officer; Sir Alfred Zimmern, professor of international relations at Oxford; Professor Heinrich von der Gablentz, political scientist from Berlin; Dr. Max Huber, Swiss, former president of the Permanent Court of International Justice; and John Foster Dulles, later to become United States Secretary of State.

It is difficult for one who has not participated in such a conference to imagine what the experience is like, what it does to the people in it, and how it reveals the nature of the Church and the churches.

These facts about the conference should be noted:

1. As Christians, we believed that it was our obligation to discover the will of God rather than to defend preconceived policies. We shared a common ground and starting point of Christian convictions underlying the various ideas we carried from our respective backgrounds of nation and tradition.

2. We had a common authority and guide in the Bible. This one fixed and accepted point provided a focus in discussions, for, despite differences of interpretation and emphasis, all recognized one source of truth to which to return.

3. We shared in Christian worship. Coming closer to God together, we came closer to one another.

4. Under such circumstances, international affairs were approached and discussed in ways quite different from those which are usual in formal relations between governments. This is not to say that the delegates at Oxford were either ill informed or indifferent with regard to the "realistic" hard cold facts of the world of practical affairs. On the contrary, among the men who led the discussions were some who were spending their lives dealing with the immediate issues as repre-

sentatives of governments, commercial and financial interests, universities, and other private agencies composed of professional experts.

The conference achieved a substantial measure of agreement. Its reports gave useful guidance to the churches. The participants returned to their respective nations and tasks with deepened insights into the problems of the world, new vision of the role of the churches, and an inspiring awareness of belonging to a vast fellowship.

While Nations Mobilized

In Geneva, in mid-July 1939, thirty-five leaders from eleven countries convened under the auspices of the Provisional Committee for the World Council of Churches. Among them were laymen who held or had held official responsibilities in connection with the Paris Peace Conference, the Reparations Commission, the Berlin Debt Conference in 1933, the London Economic Conference, the Mandates Commission of the League of Nations, the Lima Conference, governmental economic commissions, and tariff and foreign trade boards. But they came to Geneva as Christians. The tension between the nations was deeper than it had been at the time of Oxford. At one point some of the participants announced that they would leave the conference because the attitude of some members was so hostile and unjust that it was impossible for them to remain. Had it not been for the underlying Christian discipline and unity of faith, the conference would have broken up. But resort to the Bible and prayer opened us to God's power to hold us together.

A solidarity of fellowship developed. We reached agreement on a memorandum stating what the conference considered to be the responsibility of the churches in the crisis. The report was commended to the churches by the Provisional Committee, and the findings with regard to national policies were presented to the heads of some governments.

On the other side of the world, relations between the United States and Japan were deteriorating in an alarming way. Early in 1941 an urgent message came from leaders of the National Christian Council of Japan to officers of interdenominational agencies in the United States requesting a conference for the purpose of attempting to alleviate the tension.

Arrangements were made, and in April eight Christian leaders chosen by the National Christian Council of Japan met at Riverside, California, with seventeen persons from the Foreign Mission Conference and the Federal Council of Churches.

Here was another test of the bonds of Christian fellowship. Would we present and defend the list of complaints of our respective nations against each other, or would we avoid controversial issues and limit our discussions to friendly reminiscences and talk about good will? Would we mutually apologize for the bad manners or mistakes of our governments, denying our own responsibility, or would we analyze the situation realistically, honestly, frankly, but under Christian discipline?

Our consultations took the last course. By driving each other back into history, analyzing national purposes and psychological reactions, we came to a better understanding of both nations and the problems of their relationships. But we found no simple, practical, and feasible solutions to the immediate political problems.

Consequently our Bible study and prayer together became increasingly meaningful as we approached adjournment. The spiritual depth of our association was keenly felt and gratefully recognized, for we knew that separation and tragic circumstances could not change it fundamentally. In our closing sessions it was quite natural and spontaneous for us to acknowledge a solemn covenant to continue a fellowship of prayer regardless of what might happen.

We exchanged tokens of this pledge in the form of an inexpensive little silver watch-chain piece, on one side of which is the cross and bell symbol of the Mission Inn where we met, and on the reverse this simple engraving, "April 20–25, 1941." We had a prayer calendar for our common intercession and supplication. Neither the calendar nor the silver piece was necessary to seal our spiritual bond, but they became precious and useful reminders through the four tragic years of separation which followed.

Through War Itself

Our churches were overwhelmingly convinced that victory for our nation and its allies would be more in accord with the purpose of God than victory for the enemy. They exerted every effort to strengthen the moral and spiritual life of the people, but they did not presume that everything the nation might do for victory should necessarily have God's blessing.

Our churches assisted in providing a Christian ministry to prisoners of war. This was one way of transcending the lines of conflict.

After the treachery at Pearl Harbor, in the face of popular suspicion and resentment of anyone even remotely associated with Japan, the churches stood by the Japanese Americans who were abruptly evacuated from their homes and placed in improvised camps. A national church committee was organized to help make their confinement more tolerable and to assist them in resettlement.

Our churches helped to support German missionaries cut off from their home base.

Indirect communication with Christian friends in Germany and the territories it occupied was maintained through the office of the Provisional Committee for the World Council of Churches in Geneva. Personal information which meant much to us had no "security" implications and was passed by the censors.

When the Fighting Ceased

Late in 1945, the Federal Council of Churches sent Bishop G. Gromley Oxnam, its president; Dr. Franklin Clark Fry, president of the United Lutheran Church in America; and Bishop Henry Knox Sherrill, chairman of the General Commission on Army and Navy Chaplains, to Germany. The purpose of the visitation was "to seek to establish fellowship with and to ascertain the present status of the churches in Germany; to discuss with church leaders there the matter of re-establishing relationships with the churches in the United States and the possibility of co-operation between the American churches and the German churches as the latter seek to rehabilitate the spiritual life of their nation; and to discuss problems of relief and reconstruction with the American occupation authorities and the leaders of the German churches."

The report issued by the delegation on December 10, 1945, stated that its members were "fully aware of the history of this war, of the story of the concentration camps, and of the responsibility of the German leaders and people." They recalled the terrible costs of the war but declared that the very nature of the religion of Christ demanded "a wise and understanding approach to the people and more especially to the churches of Germany."

Thereafter our churches of all denominations gave generously to help the German churches in their programs of service to refugees, relief, and reconstruction.

The first American group to arrive in Japan in civilian dress after the war was sent by the Federal Council of Churches and the Foreign Missions Conference in October 1945. In the group were Dr. Douglas Horton (chairman), Bishop James C. Baker, Dr. Luman J. Shafer, and Dr. Walter W. Van Kirk.

We had been perplexed as to the best way to resume communications with Japanese Christians, from whom we had been completely shut off during the war. The problem was more complicated than the resumption of direct contact with Germany. The small Christian minority in Japan had been suspected of lack of patriotism during the war because of their history of close association with churches in enemy countries. Their religion was of "alien origin." The staggering devastation of the bombings had been inflicted by Americans. The army of occupation was American, and occupation forces are usually resented. What could American Christians do that would be helpful to Japanese Christians in that situation?

A radio broadcast from Tokyo had been picked up which assured us that the Japanese Christians would warmly welcome a visit by Americans in return for their visit to Riverside in 1941.

The American delegation reported of their first meeting with Christian leaders in Tokyo: "We shook hands briefly and said very little. Feelings ran too deep for words, but at that moment we knew that our fellowship in Christ remained unbroken, and that the cleavage in our relations occasioned by the war could be repaired and would be. We began our regular conferences with a Communion service in the Reinanzake Church."

Unfortunately the delegation's report (*The Return to Japan*, Friendship Press, New York) is out of print. It is a poignant story of Christian fellowship, of the good behavior of the army of occupation, and the friendliness of the people. I quote an episode to illustrate that Christian unity is not limited to church leaders:

"One young G.I., entering the city of Tokyo on a Sunday with the first echelon of troops and having time on his hands that afternoon, looked about for a church to worship in. On the horizon the steeple of the Reinanzake Church was discernible. Making his way through the devastation, he finally reached the church, and, entering it, found himself in the midst of a meeting where a serious discussion was in progress. One of those present, seeing him come in, slipped over to the pew where he sat and bade him welcome, in English. He told him that this was a meeting of the representatives of churches of the entire Tokyo district discussing what their first steps should be, now that the war was over.

"As the young man listened to the speeches, translated to him by his companion, he grew more and more moved—and finally rose and said, 'No one sent me here but the Holy Spirit—but I am a Baptist from Chicago, and I want to bring you the greetings of the Protestant churches of America.' Now it was the turn of the others to be moved. They had not known what his purpose had been in coming to the meeting—but his brief speech proclaimed him a friend. They appointed one of their elder leaders to give him a formal greeting and extend to him the right hand of fellowship."

Thus it can be seen that from the Geneva and Riverside conferences on the eve of World War II, during the war period, and through the renewal of direct association with German and Japanese Christians immediately after the cessation of fighting, the bonds of Christian unity were progressively deepened. The churches became more and more one fellowship. By the organizing of the World Council of Churches in 1948, the fellowship was given a corporate expression and instrument to facilitate communication and to enable the member churches to act together in witness and service to their one Lord.

Relief and Reconstruction

Another major aspect of the progress in Christian unity was the growth of a vast program of relief and reconstruction. Even before the war ended, the Provisional Committee for the World Council of Churches had set up an organization through which the churches could help one another in the aftermath of unprecedented devastation and also serve people in need regardless of their nationality or religion.

Those who gave sacrificially through their churches found joy in helping. Those who received knew that Christianity meant more than words. The value of the tangible saving of lives was obvious. But it was of immeasurable importance to millions in despair to learn that Christian people cared.

Hope was restored by acts of compassion. During the period when many in Europe were utterly demoralized in an existence of futility and boredom, wondering whether there would be a tomorrow for them, the arrival of help from unknown faraway friends in the name of Christ prevented spiritual and mental as well as physical disaster.

This program had been planned during the war by the Provisional Committee for the World Council and put into operation as soon as opportunities opened. Thus it was a large enterprise before the World Council was formally constituted in 1948.

The Commission of the Churches on International Affairs

Immediately after the war it was recognized that the churches needed an agency to help them to exert a more effective influence in the field of international affairs. The development of mutual understanding among the churches of many nations provided the basis for an organization to serve their common interests.

Consequently, the Provisional Committee for the World Council of Churches and the International Missionary Council joined in sponsoring an international conference on world order in the summer of 1946 and in authorizing it to establish the Commission of the Churches on International Affairs (C.C.I.A.).

Sixty delegates from fifteen nations, some recently at war with each other, met at Cambridge University in England. John Foster Dulles was chairman of the conference. It was keenly aware of the importance of its task. It declared in the preamble to the charter of the C.C.I.A.: "Since the invention of the atomic bomb the problem of peace has acquired unprecedented urgency. No one knows how much time is given to mankind to find a way out of the political and economic conflicts of our day into an order of mutual trust and stable peace. But we do know that if the nations do not find a way of regulating their relationships we are doomed to mutual destruction."

It defined the responsibilities of the churches: "To interpret the Will of God in relation to the tangled problems of world politics and economics is a formidable task demanding accurate information and prudent judgment as well as spiritual insight. It is an inescapable duty of the Church at the present hour to contribute to those who bear responsibility in these fields the aid of Christian perspectives and to remind them of Christian imperatives."

The primary function assigned to the C.C.I.A. was that of "serving the churches, councils, and conferences which are members of the World Council of Churches and the International Missionary Council as a source of stimulus and knowledge in their approach to international problems, as a medium of common counsel and action, and as their organ in formulating the Christian mind on world issues and in bringing that mind effectively to bear upon them."

Professor Baron F. F. van Asbeck of the Netherlands, experienced in government and international administration, became the first president. Sir Kenneth Grubb of the United Kingdom has been chairman since the beginning, and Dr. O. Frederick Nolde of the United States, director.

The Commission has had a membership of about forty men and women from twenty-five or more countries. A large majority of them have been laymen with professional experience in public life. Some 250 correspondents in more than seventy countries help to keep the Commission informed and advised with regard to developments in practically all corners of the world.

Officers of the Commission travel long distances on short notice to consult church leaders in situations of tension and to remind governments of the concerns of the churches. They are present at nearly all important world conferences of diplomats and attend most meetings of the United Nations General Assembly and Security Council. All important developments in the United Nations and its specialized agencies are reported to the churches.

Public services of intercession are frequently arranged by the Commission in a nearby church when important international conferences are assembled. The diplomats know that their efforts to solve problems are supported by prayer.

The Commission has been especially interested in human rights and religious liberty, technical assistance to underdeveloped countries, the work of the United Nations Trusteeship Council, the Food and Agriculture Organization, and the World Health Organization.

On the basis of its study, long experience, and the expressed views of the churches, the Commission occasionally submits careful analyses and recommends statements of position to the Central Committee of the World Council of Churches. When such statements have been considered and approved—often after amendment—they provide a basis of authorization for the continuing work of the Commission and help the various churches to see international problems in an ecumenical perspective.

Thus the C.C.I.A. helps Christians to bring their convictions to bear on international affairs in two ways. First, they are provided with an agency through which as church members they can forcefully call Christian principles to the attention of leaders at the point of decision; and second, they receive expert, reliable interpretation from a Christian point of view which helps them as citizens to exert a Christian influence on public opinion and governmental processes.

The average reader may not be aware of his relationship to the C.C.I.A. It may seem remote. So do Congress and the State Department. In both instances the representative principle and process prevail. Anyone who is a member of a church which is a member of the World Council of Churches is related to the C.C.I.A. through his church.

Across the "Cold War" Lines

During the entire period of the consolidation of the fellowship of the churches since World War I there remained always a "vacant chair." The churches in our country had almost no association with the churches in the Soviet Union. There had been little earlier association to be restored. Even before the revolution of 1917 the Orthodox Church of Russia had been rather isolated from the West. The leadership of that period had been liquidated and a new generation was now on the scene.

The governments of the two nations had been in tension for most of this period except during World War II. But with the beginning of the Korean War, if not earlier, the psychological truce had ended and the menace of communism had become the absorbing problem of our nation's foreign policy.

It seemed to be imperative that our American churches should at least make an attempt to enter into association with the leaders of the churches in the Soviet Union. Two interrelated concerns impelled us: transcending the barriers that separated us from professing Christians living under an atheistic totalitarian regime, and building a bridge between peoples in order to start discussions in the interest of international understanding.

These concerns were so urgent as to outweigh the obvious and complex difficulties we knew we would encounter. The General Board of the National Council of Churches therefore authorized a deputation to be sent to the churches in the Soviet Union. The delegation was composed of Dr. Eugene Carson Blake (chairman), Mr. Paul B. Anderson, Dr. Franklin Clark Fry, Dr. Herbert Gezork, Bishop D. Ward Nichols, Mr. Charles C. Parlin, Rt. Rev. Henry Knox Sherrill, Dr. Walter W. Van Kirk, and Dr. Roswell P. Barnes. Mr. Donald C. Bolles was the public relations officer.

Despite discouraging initial responses from the Soviet Embassy in Washington, and after long delays, clearance was finally obtained from the two governments and direct correspondence opened with the designated officer of the Holy Orthodox Church in Moscow, Metropolitan Nicholai.

In his speeches at the meetings of the communist-denominated World Peace Conference, as they had been reported in the press and published in the journal of the Moscow Patriarchate, the Metropolitan had clearly followed the propaganda line of the Kremlin. We knew that we would have an opportunity to deal with real issues and to confront men who were in positions of effective leadership. (The use of "we" as applied to the deputation is "editorial" when it involves appraisal or judgment in the course of the narrative. I alone am responsible for the opinions expressed.)

We knew that we would face a difficult but authentic test of the principle of unity in Christ. We also knew that we would have the opportunity to learn much.

As we projected ourselves by imagination into the situation, fundamental questions began to take form in my mind as considerations to be remembered in the conversations soon to take place: At what points does loyalty to one's nation become incompatible with loyalty to Christ? Can one be loyal to his nation without being loyal to the government in power in the nation? What is one's moral responsibility for the positions he takes in the light of the only facts and interpretations available to him on the one side through controlled channels of information and on the other side through nationally prejudiced channels? How can one Christian judge whether another who takes the name of Christ is sincere in his profession? Does one Christian judge another Christian's *motives?* Can we say that we have Christian fellowship if we do not judge one another's words and deeds? Should a Christian compromise in order to be allowed to bear some witness, or should he defy and take prison or death, or should he try to flee to freedom? When should ministers and priests abandon their flocks?

We approached association with the leaders of the churches in the Soviet Union in a mood of humility before very basic questions, with a sense of grave responsibility because of what the venture meant for the Church of Christ and for the cause of peace, and—most significantly—in dependence upon God because, recognizing our own inability by our own wisdom to "handle the situation," we looked to Him for guidance and strength.

When we arrived in Moscow in March 1956, we were confident that we were there in obedience to our faith that this is God's world, that He came into it in history uniquely in Christ, and that if the world is to be saved it is through Christ, who offered reconciliation of men to God and to one another. We had not checked our minds at the airport, nor did we think that we could solve all problems by our own unaided intelligence. Our dependence upon God in prayer was more obvious, articulate, and complete than it is usually.

Our hosts and the other church leaders seemed strange to us—as we doubtless did to them—in many obvious ways: garb, beards, and language, for example. Only one of our deputation understood the Russian language—Dr. Paul B. Anderson, who not only understood it but was so proficient as to be able to catch its inner meaning. None of the churchmen with whom we normally talked had any knowledge of English beyond the rudiments. We relied largely on interpreters.

Baptists were present for most of our discussions, also Lutherans from the Baltic states and Armenians. They seemed less strange in appearance and manners. But the Russian Orthodox who were our official hosts were quite different from the church people with whom we are accustomed to associate around our conference tables.

For most of those with whom we talked, this was the first discussion on matters of religion with Christians from overseas, from the United States, at least. The members of our deputation were experienced in ecumenical encounter in other settings, but for them this was the first of its kind. Understanding each other's ideas was not easy.

Despite all these barriers, some of us did communicate with one another. We did have fellowship. It was not our achievement. But God was among us. We knew it. Though our words and observable behavior had to be circumspect, genuine Christian rapport was achieved.

Even so, just when we would seem to be reaching a mutual understanding, a crucial difference in judgment with regard to the world situation would arise. The difficulties of communicating ideas at Geneva in 1939 or at Riverside in 1941 were trivial in comparison with the difficulties in Moscow in 1956.

The pendulum seemed to swing between success and failure regarding the specific items on our agenda. But in the general situation, the relations between two groups of Christians, there was no doubt. In the Soviet Union were people who were dedicated to Christ and were living out their faith according to the centuries-old tradition of their churches. We came to know another side of Metropolitan Nicholai.

As our conversations progressed, we came to a better mutual understanding at many points. Occasionally we reached agreements. But it did not disturb us too much if we did not arrive at agreements so long as we understood each other enough to be able to define and clarify our disagreements. This is not to say that we were content to define our disagreements, for we were uneasy about them. The important consideration is that we had a better sense of community as we came to understand each other's positions than we had had when we attributed positions to sheer obstinacy or perverseness. The distinction between understanding and agreement is highly important.

Despite all doubts and the feeling of distance at many points, we came to share in common testimony to the sovereignty and the saving grace of God. We acknowledged together our faith in the leadership of the Holy Spirit. We engaged in common worship. We joined in the adoration of God in their services in their churches. Genuine piety and sincere profession of faith in the face of an atheistic totalitarian and pervasive governmental power were unquestionable. There were manifestations of authentic Christian commitment in the churches.

Being convinced of that fact, we were challenged and inspired. We hope that our presence among them was used of God to confirm their faith and strengthen their testimony.

When a group of those with whom we had associated in the Soviet Union came to the United States three months later to return our visit, our conviction of basic Christian fellowship was confirmed and deepened. Disagreements on many points persisted, but we were increasingly certain that God had given us a unity in Christ on the basis of which we could build understanding.

A bridge had been built. Some dangerous people who live by their antagonisms, confusing hatred of people with loyalty to principle, resent the bridge and seek to destroy it. It is only a footbridge, but we hope that as God strengthens the faith of those on both sides of the chasm a structure adequate to carry heavier traffic can be built. There have been numerous other exchanges of visits between church leaders from other countries and those in the Soviet Union. The Russian Orthodox Church has been studying the World Council of Churches. It sent observers to the meeting of the Central Committee of the World Council in 1959, and a staff delegation from the Council visited the churches in the Soviet Union in December of that year to discuss means for furthering mutual acquaintance.

CHAPTER V

Major Social Problem Areas

We come now to an analysis of the role and actions of the churches in some of the major problem areas of public affairs.

International Relations and Foreign Policy

What are international relations?

In a narrow and rather technical sense, they are relations between national governments. Governments deal with one another either singly, or collectively as parts of a community of nations in an inter-governmental agency such as the United Nations. In the former pattern they operate through their diplomatic agents to arrive at agreements on matters of mutual concern. In the latter pattern they work through their representatives in a world organization in association with delegates from many nations.

In a broader and more basic sense, international relations are relations not between governments but rather between peoples. Nations are masses of people. Governments are agencies acting for nations. Therefore, governments generally represent in some measure the will of their people, varying from a large measure in the case of the democratic governments to an almost negligible measure in totalitarian states. Even in the latter, however, the governments are not entirely divorced from the will of the people, for they seek to influence and control public attitudes so as to increase acceptance, if not support, for their policies and practices. Consequently, any contact or communication between people across national boundaries may have some bearing on the relations between their nations.

All persons are important in international relations, from the heads of state to the man in the street. The Summit Conference in Paris in 1960, abandoned before it could begin, was an important act in the drama of world affairs. Nations were the principals. But is it not unrealistic to think only of nations as abstract, legalistic, corporate entities? What are nations?

Consider the role of people as individual persons in this drama. President Eisenhower, Premier Khrushchev, Prime Minister Macmillan, and President de Gaulle were on the stage because of what they represented and symbolized. But what they did, the way in which they did it, their personalities, their facial expressions, their gestures were the expressions of persons as well as the definitions of national policies. In such a situation, nations are symbolized by persons, for the persons who symbolically and legally represent nations are still persons. Moreover, the nations they represent are masses of persons.

Congressional committees, the editors of our newspapers and magazines, the commentators on radio and television, the units of the public whose opinions are sampled by the reporters, all are persons. These make up the "public opinion" which is the nation.

Persons are therefore the obvious factors and also the power behind the scenes in international affairs. They seem to be submerged and futile in modern mass society. But in the final analysis they still count.

Thus it is of the utmost importance, in considering the relations of the churches to international affairs, to keep clearly in mind the distinction between the narrow or technical and the broader aspects of international affairs—the distinction between the state and the nation, the government and the people, the technical and the psychological, the scientific and the moral, the impersonal and the personal. But the two sets of factors should not be separated. While the distinctions are useful for purposes of analysis, their close relationship is also important. For example, the codification of international law and the development of a common ethos among the peoples go hand in hand. The negotiation of tariff agreements—a highly technical task—is futile unless the government will ratify and the people support the necessary enabling measures. An international convention on human rights would be of little value without the will of the people of the nations to support it.

Such reasoning leads us to the conclusion that whatever influences the people in one country in their attitudes toward people in other countries influences international affairs. The churches, therefore, influence international affairs by influencing people, both those in leadership who symbolize nations and those who comprise the public opinions of nations.

The basic factors in the influence of the churches on international relations were discussed in Chapter IV. I turn now to the concerted efforts of the churches to make Christian principles and conviction effective in public opinion and national policy.

After World War I the United States had turned its back on the League of Nations and withdrawn into isolationism. Early in World War II it was realized that we might do the same thing again after the fighting was over. The Federal Council of Churches in 1940 constituted the Commission on a Just and Durable Peace, with John Foster Dulles as chairman, to help the churches make an effective contribution to world order, justice, and peace immediately and in preparation for the post-war period.

The Commission began its work with a careful examination of the teachings of the Christian faith with regard to the problems before it. This required basic analysis by theologians, historians, and statesmen. A set of Guiding Principles for history and human relations was formulated and submitted to a national study conference of delegates from the churches. After revision and amplification in explanatory texts, they were given widespread study in the churches. This was the first step in a well-planned program. Every word of the statement of Guiding Principles was well considered.

The points of that statement (abbreviated) should be noted:

Preamble

As members of the Christian Church, we seek to view all problems of world order in the light of the truth concerning God, man and God's purpose for the world made known in Jesus Christ. We believe that the eternal God revealed in Christ is the Ruler of men and of nations and that His purpose in history will be realized. For us He is the source of moral law and the power to make it effective.

Guiding Principles

1. We believe that moral law, no less than physical law, undergirds our world.

2. We believe that the sickness and suffering which afflict our present society are proof of indifference to, as well as direct violation of, the moral law.

3. We believe that it is contrary to the moral order that nations in their dealings with one another should be motivated by a spirit of revenge and retaliation.

4. We believe that the principle of co-operation and mutual concern,

implicit in the moral order and essential to a just and durable peace, calls for a true community of nations.

5. We believe that economic security is no less essential than political security to a just and durable peace.

6. We believe that international machinery is required to facilitate the easing of such economic and political tensions as are inevitably recurrent in a world which is living and therefore changing.

7. We believe that that government which derives its just powers from the consent of the governed is the truest expression of the rights and dignity of man.

8. We believe that military establishments should be internationally controlled and be made subject to law under the community of nations.

9. We believe that the right of all men to pursue work of their own choosing and to enjoy security from want and oppression is not limited by race, color or creed.

10. We believe that, in bringing international relations into conformity with the moral law, a very heavy responsibility devolves upon the United States.

11. We believe that, as Christian citizens, we must seek to translate our beliefs into practical realities and to create a public opinion which will insure that the United States shall play its full and essential part in the creation of a moral way of international living.

12. We believe that a supreme responsibility rests with the Church. The Church, being a creation of God in Jesus Christ, is called to proclaim to all men everywhere the way of life. Moreover, the Church which is now in reality a world community, may be used of God to develop His spirit of righteousness and love in every race and nation and thus to make possible a just and durable peace.

The Guiding Principles were taken seriously by the churches and generally recognized to be sound and important. But they were, intentionally, basic generalizations; and their relevance to practical problems of foreign policy was not apparent to most people. The next step—begun as soon as the Guiding Principles were published—was to formulate a series of propositions setting forth the implications of the basic principles for international relations and world order. They were statements of "middle axioms," halfway between the generalizations and the specific measures upon which governments must make decisions. They became widely known as the Six Pillars of Peace:

1. The peace must provide the political framework for a continuing collaboration of the United Nations and, in due course, of neutral and enemy nations.

2. The peace must make provision for bringing within the scope of

international agreements those economic and financial acts of national governments which have widespread international repercussions.

3. The peace must make provision for an organization to adapt the treaty structure of the world to changing underlying conditions.

4. The peace must proclaim the goal of autonomy for subject peoples, and it must establish international organization to assure and to supervise the realization of that end.

5. The peace must establish procedures for controlling military establishments everywhere.

6. The peace must establish in principle, and seek to achieve in practice, the right of individuals everywhere to religious and intellectual liberty.

Articles by eminent authorities, widely published, interpreted the relevance of the Pillars to the problems of the world. Study documents were issued. Churches across the country gave earnest attention to the Principles and the Pillars. The secular press carried the news and editorial comment, usually favorable.

The churches were thus being rallied and mobilized to change the climate of public opinion. Roman Catholic and Jewish agencies made similar efforts, and a statement was issued simultaneously by the three faiths over the names of nationally respected leaders. This collaboration was unprecedented.

The White House, the State Department, and Congress heard from the people and became aware of a moral mandate for United States initiative on behalf of responsible international organization for peaceful change, world order, justice, and freedom.

This was probably the most effective and impressive exertion of influence by the churches and Christian citizens on United States foreign policy in our history.

Soon after that period, Mr. Dulles said in an address at the Washington Cathedral, on March 11, 1948:

"Internationally and nationally, the churches have organized themselves to put the impress of Christian thinking upon the life of nations. That effort is already showing positive results.

"It was the Christian churches of America that in 1941 took the initiative in demanding that, after this war, there should be a world organization in which the United States would participate. That peace aim had been omitted from the Atlantic Charter because President Roosevelt and Prime Minister Churchill feared that the prevalent American mood was still that which 20 years before had rejected the League of Nations. Whether or not they were right at the moment, they were not right for long. The churches saw to that. They conducted

intensively throughout this land national missions and study groups
on world order, with the result that our political leaders knew that
they were following the popular will when, two years after the Atlantic
Charter, they made world organization an added peace objective."

As Mr. Dulles intimated, the impetus of the churches' effort and their
acquired familiarity with the issues were such that when the Dumbarton
Oaks draft charter for the United Nations Organization was issued
they were prepared to give it judicious analysis. They detected certain
deficiencies and proposed amendments—not in specific formulation but
in substance. Notably they urged that more adequate provision be
made for safeguarding human rights and assisting non-self-governing
territories to make progress toward independence.

Meanwhile churches in other countries had been conducting studies
similar to those initiated by the Commission on a Just and Durable
Peace, in some instances using our publications. Before the San
Francisco conference at which the United Nations Organization was
constituted, the churches in numerous nations had approached their
delegates and expressed concern at some of the points that had troubled
us. At San Francisco provision was made for the Human Rights Commission and for the Trusteeship Council.

Other illustrations of points at which the churches have exerted
influence on United States foreign policy are: legislation regarding
displaced persons and refugees, immigration policy affecting Asians,
and technical assistance to peoples in underdeveloped countries. Influence has been exerted by Christian citizens expressing their convictions
to their representatives and leaders in Washington. Their concern has
also been interpreted in person to the President, the State Department,
and congressional committees by national leaders of the churches—
laymen and ministers—under authorization of the National Council
of Churches and the several denominations, and by arrangements
made by the Department of International Affairs.

Race Relations

Hate and love, fear and hope, resentment and good will, prejudice
and fairness, restlessness and patience—these are the spiritual and
psychological ingredients of the race problem.

The emergence of peoples of color into independent nationhood,
world-wide alignments of common interests, rapid social change,
discriminatory laws, long-established patterns of segregation, consol-
idations of group power in rebellion or resistance, the increasing
interrelatedness of all groups of mankind—these are the social factors

of challenge, aggressiveness, and resistance in which and through which the dynamic and often demonic spiritual and psychological forces are in tension or open conflict.

Most international issues complicate or are complicated by race problems. Race is also an aspect of many tensions within our own country—a minor plot within the major plot of the drama of our national life and destiny.

The situation alarms and baffles us as a people, partly because it is so complex and partly because technology, on which we have relied too much for solutions to all our problems, cannot help us much. For the elements involved in the race problem are motives, feelings, inner disciplines, pride, selfishness, ambition for our own kind, and other sins; suffering, redemption, and reconciliation. These are beyond technology. These are the business of the churches. The churches have claimed them appropriately as their field of competence and responsibility.

The secularists who profess no religious faith and many nominal Christians watch—some skeptically, some wistfully—hoping that the churches may provide the difference between success and failure in dealing with the problem.

In this country, despite the occasional magazine article or other accusation that eleven o'clock on Sunday morning is the most segregated hour of the week, there seems to be a general public gratitude for the leadership the churches have taken. Their public statements of principle are regarded as news. When leaders identified with the church take a stand that shows courage and a willingness to sacrifice career, popularity, and security, they are gratefully recognized in the nation as a whole. Though roundly condemned by those they have opposed, they are usually respected. There has been widespread appreciation, in some quarters not expressed, for the spiritual and moral discipline, insight, and integrity of most Negro church leaders and the people who have rallied around them.

As in international relations, so also in race relations, progress in Christian unity has had its effect on the attitudes and behavior of church members. Common faith reaches across both national and racial boundaries. So for Christians, race relations are not only a matter of ethics, sociology, economics, and politics but also a matter of fellowship within the community of the church.

This is a point at which the nature of the church is crucial. A church that assumes it is free to formulate its fundamental policy on race forgets what it is or denies its own nature; its guiding principles are given in the Bible. It is under orders. Its only choice is with regard to the application of its given principles in practice. The latitude of choice for it is not nearly as broad as it is for secular voluntary organizations. The majority opinion of the community is not an appropriate guide for a church. The Bible and theological analyses are more basic authorities for the Christian than the findings of anthropology and sociology, though social science is helpful at the point of applying principle to practice.

An Ecumenical Process

The Evanston Assembly of the World Council of Churches in 1954 provides a useful illustration of the formulation of a statement of basic Christian principle and policy. One of the sections of the Assembly was assigned the task of dealing with "The Church amid Racial and Ethnic Tensions."

A preparatory commission, set up two years in advance, made a systematic inquiry of the churches in various nations to discover the problems they faced, the patterns of race relations in their several countries, and the positions and practices of the churches. Laws were examined, and the research findings of governments, universities, and United Nations agencies were analyzed.

A year before the Assembly, the commission met for a week in Geneva to study the results of the inquiry and to prepare a background document which the delegates to the Assembly were expected to study in preparation for making responsible decisions. The insights of theology, anthropology, sociology, and church administration were brought forth by members of the commission, who came from Africa, Asia, Europe, and America. Drafting, discussing, and rewriting continued day after day.

In the course of this thorough and careful work we found ourselves constantly going back to the Bible as our common authority. Difference of theological analysis and conflicting ideas concerning the role of the church in the world divided us until we went back to the source and found agreement on the basic tenets of our faith. We were surprised to discover how much we had unconsciously used theology to rationalize and justify our several national positions. The background document therefore emphasized biblical teachings, basic theological principles, and an exposition of the nature of the church.

When the section of the Assembly at Evanston went to work to produce a statement for the Assembly to consider and, it was hoped, commend to the churches, it had before it the background paper which the churches had had an opportunity to study. However, the section was not bound in any way by that paper nor by anything else that had been thought or said before. It was free to express itself. The members did, of course, feel an obligation—in their representative capacity as delegates—to take into serious consideration the position of their respective churches.

Early in the discussions, conflicting opinions and convictions emerged. Tensions soon came into the open. There were Africans—both Negro and white—including Anglican and Dutch Reformed churchmen from South Africa; Asians; Europeans; and Negroes and whites from the United States, both North and South. There were also Germans—including Dr. Martin Niemoeller—with the vivid, poignant memory of Hitler's racism, and church leaders from areas where communists and Moslems sneer at Christianity because its churches practice or condone racial segregation and discrimination.

Such wide and divergent backgrounds and experiences are a characteristic of a truly ecumenical group. (One wonders whether any national group can appropriately regard itself ecumenical. It can be such in purpose and spirit, but not in experience.) These were all Christian leaders. But they were also citizens of nations having varying histories and problems. They were all identified to some extent with particular cultures, each having a sense of its own value and destiny.

The differences became acute. Objective discussion changed to debate at times. (Who can distinguish between temper and deep convictions?) We were all in a way dual personalities: we were church members and also Christian citizens deeply involved in national and cultural heritages and loyalties. Neither could be denied. Which would prevail? Were the two necessarily antagonistic?

We were faced with the crucial problem of how to deal with differences of judgment. Is the basic problem that of eliminating the differences or of finding a way of recognizing them without accepting them as final, achieving mutual understanding, and thus establishing a relationship within which they may be progressively reduced both in substance and in tension?

The situation was beyond resolution by mere human ingenuity, courage, or good will. That was so obvious that we became humble, for we desired to be obedient to Christ. Worship became a truly spiritual act. We came closer together in such a mood that we sought and awaited the leadership of the Holy Spirit. Then our calling as Christians became paramount. We became—by God's grace and power—a group of fellow Christians within the Church, conscious of the meaning of the Church and of a church. We were then different from an intergovernmental or any other secular group. Although we were not bound by anything which had been said by any groups before, we felt bound by the Bible and by our agreed theological principles.

Some of the members of the section had come to the Assembly prepared to withdraw from the World Council of Churches if it should take a position on race contrary to their own. Speeches explaining such withdrawal had been prepared in advance. They were abandoned, not because of any parliamentary pressure, but because of the experience of, and the realization of, the true meaning of membership in the Church of Jesus Christ.

Under such circumstances, the report produced by the section was especially significant. Its basic affirmation with regard to the calling of the Church and individual Christians was this:

This is the calling of the Church with regard to race, to witness within itself to the Kingship of Christ and the unity of His people, in Him transcending all diversity. Jesus Christ in His Incarnation and redemptive action restores this unity which from the beginning was God's design.

Their calling requires Christians to witness to the Kingship of Christ and the unity of all mankind, and to strive through social and political action to secure justice, freedom, and peace for all, as a foretaste of the Kingdom into which the faithful shall be gathered.

All churches and Christians are involved, whether they recognize it or not, in the racial and ethnic tensions of the world. But it is in communities where segregation prevails that they face the plainest difficulties and the most challenging opportunities; for such segregation denies to those who are segregated their just and equal rights and results in deep injuries to the human spirit, suffered by offender and victim alike.

In speaking of the task of the churches, the report said:

The churches have this twofold duty, to obey and to proclaim the word of judgment, to repent and to call to repentance. It is their task to challenge the conscience of society; if there is no tension between the church and society, then either the society is regenerate or the church is conformed. Yet it also has a duty to create and to keep open every possible line of communication between people, between political opponents, between people of differing views, cultures, races, languages, between the conservative and the venturesome.

The report was received by the Assembly and commended by it to the churches "for study and appropriate action." The section also recommended several resolutions to the Assembly for its adoption.

By its approval, they became an official policy statement of the World Council of Churches, including the following commitment:

The Second Assembly of the World Council of Churches declares its conviction that any form of segregation based on race, color, or ethnic origin is contrary to the Gospel, and is incompatible with the Christian doctrine of man and with the nature of the Church of Christ. The Assembly urges the churches within its membership to renounce all forms of segregation or discrimination and to work for their abolition within their own life and within society.

In doing so the Assembly is painfully aware that, in the realities of the contemporary world, many churches find themselves confronted by historical, political, social, and economic circumstances which may make the immediate achievement of this objective extremely difficult. But under God the fellowship of the ecumenical movement is such as to offer to these churches the strength and encouragement to help them and individuals within them to overcome those difficulties with the courage given by faith, and with the desire to testify ever more faithfully to our Master.

Several members of the Assembly abstained from voting on the resolution and entered an explanation of their reasons for doing so. Their rights were recognized and respected. This was further evidence of the kind of fellowship that prevailed.

No other occasion in my rather extensive experience has done so much as that Evanston section to make me grateful and confident that the power of the Holy Spirit is available among humble and obedient servants of Jesus Christ. And I doubt whether such results could have been attained if we had not gone back to the Bible and our basic theological beliefs for authoritative guidance.

After the Assembly, many of the churches gave careful attention to the section's report and the resolutions. In South Africa more effective co-operation was achieved between the churches that had previously found it difficult to work together. In the United States the principles of the Evanston statements were generally accepted by the churches.

Actions by the United States Churches

Even before the World Council's action, our churches had been turning increasingly to the Bible and theology and had come to positions similar to those taken at Evanston. The Federal Council of Churches had committed itself unequivocally against discrimination in 1946. Many of the denominations had been taking similar positions. On June 11, 1952, the General Board of the National Council of Churches said:

The National Council of the churches of Christ in the U.S.A., in its organizational structure and operation, renounces and earnestly recommends to its member churches that they renounce the pattern of segregation based on race, color or national origin as unnecessary and undesirable and a violation of the Gospel of love and human brotherhood.

The Methodist Church, after a series of regional studies, held a national Conference on Human Relations in 1959 in which ten agencies of the church co-operated. Its approach to the problem of race is worthy of note. Its primary stated purpose was "to face objectively and concretely the perplexing issues of race relations through biblical and theological study, sound sociological analysis, exchange with experts, group discussion, able addresses, and spiritual enrichment by music, drama and the Holy Communion."

The Message of the Conference, consistent with its statement of purpose, starts with "The Basis of Our Witness" as found in the Bible. Theological propositions lead to this: "Christian love makes imperative the elimination of the injustices and inhumanities associated with present-day race relations. Full fellowship with the Father is impossible unless we accept this obligation of inclusive love for all men. Our decisions concerning race are thus basically related to our eternal salvation."

The Message includes specific recommendations with regard to housing, education, employment, and the church; but its most significant feature, in my opinion, is its relating our behavior in race relations to "our eternal salvation."

Most of the churches in their actions are repeatedly pointing to the fact that race relations are not so much a matter of social expedience as of religious faith. Theology has more of the basic answers than anthropology, sociology, and economics. Redemptive suffering is more important than knowledge and skill.

The churches are beginning to realize and teach that the spiritual consequences of inflicting suffering are more devastating than those of enduring suffering. The fences men build to shield themselves against others become walls that imprison.

Thus, their first action is to proclaim the Word of God. That gives the understanding and discipline which help us to stand by people when the issue is hot. One minister spent almost one entire night with a state church executive "as he tried to head off a serious race riot, shuttling back and forth from police to press to leaders of the two groups to the actual scene of potential disruption, where he quietly and

symbolically reached out and took a weapon from one of the leaders."
Some churches resist the use of their facilities by private schools seeking
to evade court orders to desegregate public schools. Others aid ministers in financial need as a result of their stand on race or help to
relocate them. One group paid hospital and doctor bills for a minister
beaten by the Klan.

For another example of local action I quote from a program leaflet
of the Council for Social Action, Congregational Christian Churches:

"St. Louis rezoned a residential block on the 'white side' of a
racial population line in the heart of town. The gracious, substantial
single-family houses on the shady street could not be remodeled as
two-family dwellings. Immediately, 'For Sale' signs appeared in front
yards all down the street. More signs went up when two Negro families
moved into the block.

"Samuel H. Marcus had a 16-room colonial brick house in the block.
Soon a sign went up on his lawn. The lettering was large, and unmis-
takable in meaning: 'This house is not for sale. We like our fine
neighbors. Your race, religion and politics are not our concern. All
who take pride in their homes are welcome on this street.'

"There were six 'For Sale' signs in neighborhood yards when Mr.
Marcus erected his. Shortly thereafter all were removed."

The General Board of the National Council of Churches in June
1960 pointed out the elements of Christian witness in the disciplined
behavior of many of the young people engaged in the "sit-in" protests
against segregation at lunch counters. In an article in the New York
Times on March 6, 1960, surveying "The Mood of the South" from
Atlanta, Claude Sitton said, "Aside from a few lay groups in the race
relations field, the churches have been virtually the only white organizations to endorse the demonstrations."

Mr. Harold C. Fleming, director of the Southern Regional Council,
said in Atlanta that there was no organized force of comparable size
doing as much for racial amity and integration as the churches.
Potentially, he said, it is a tremendous force, if it can be brought
down to the local level.

Such tributes are gratifying. Let us hope they are merited. But we
have no cause for complacency. The churches conform to the prevailing pattern of the community in some respects nearly everywhere,
and in many respects in some places. Our record should be much
better; for race relations, because of the nature of the problem, are a
special responsibility of the churches.

Our Practices and Our World Influence

Our policy and actions should be determined primarily by our faith and our understanding of the nature and role of the church. But the exigencies of historical situations should be taken into consideration, for God may speak to us through history. Christian values and purposes are at stake in the world situation. Our national conduct with regard to race has a very definite and important bearing upon what influence we as a people can exert in the world community. Our words about justice and freedom are flung back into our faces when our deeds deny our preaching.

I have been scrupulously careful not to make public the substance of pastoral conversations, but there is one discussion with the late John Foster Dulles which was more professional than personal which I believe he would want me to relate.

It was in the office of the Secretary of State. Mr. Dulles was pacing the floor, perturbed, frustrated, and somewhat resentful. He was giving a lecture to me as a church official. I, representing in his mind at the moment the church, was responsible for making his job impossible. He could not make the speech he wanted to make in the United Nations Assembly about freedom and justice because he would face the retort: "What about the Negro in the United States?" It was the churches' fault. The churches had fallen down. If they had fulfilled their responsibility we could now hold before the world an example of the principles we profess. He himself had been deeply involved—partly through my persuasion—in a successful effort of the churches to help to take the country out of isolation into leadership for world organization for peace, freedom, and justice. He believed that if the churches would take the problem of race as seriously they could change the national disposition. He was realistic enough to recognize that his problem was more difficult, but he was desperately in earnest in pleading that we make a much greater effort.

Conviction and loyalty combined to deepen my resolve to do more. But race was a "controversial matter." The churches were being accused of being "red." A senator from a state in which the churches were raising questions, not wanting to antagonize his own constituents in the churches but wanting to discount their influence, accused the National Council of Churches of being "red" because it meddled in the race problem and thus played the communist game. How ironical it is that some of the people who talk loudest about their opposition to communism are the communists' best allies by confirming their indictment of democracy.

At last it can be said that the conscience of the churches has been disturbed and that the right questions, searching questions, are being raised. The Rev. Will Campbell speaks from poignant and redemptive experience when he says:

Some of the best preaching I have heard has wrestled, not with the anthropological question, "What is race?" but with the theological questions, "What is the Church?" and "What is the nature of the Christian faith?" And it is more than possible that these two questions are more relevant to the crisis than the first. And certainly when they are asked by such dark-skinned people as Elizabeth Eckford in a mob-possessed schoolyard when her only protector and comforter was a woman accused by a congressional committee of being a communist. Or when they are asked by the spirit of Mack Charles Parker as he is dragged from the waters of the muddy Pearl. . . . When these questions are asked by voices it is more than an academic question to be considered in seminary halls and faith and order conferences. It is a question to be asked by everyone wearing the sign of the cross.

Economic Life

Those who tell the churches not to meddle in the problems of economic life often claim that it is a field controlled by technical laws about which the churches know nothing. To a certain extent this is true, but if the statement is not analyzed it may be used as a pretext to deny moral responsibility in important sections of life.

The social science of economics deals, for example, with units of consumption; but those units are usually human beings. A man in his economic function and capacity is still a man, and the churches are concerned with anything that effects the lives of men, women, and children. The farmer, banker, machinist, plant manager, union officer, or clerk is still a man, whether on the job or elsewhere.

Housing involves technical factors of supply and demand, costs of construction and maintenance, depreciation, interest on capital investment, insurance, and other such matters. Housing also involves the health, family life, and morals of people. Society is therefore concerned. Politics and corruption in public administration often come into play. Thus economics becomes all mixed up with a great variety of considerations.

The Rev. James Gusweiler, an Episcopal clergyman whose parish is in a deteriorating neighborhood on the west side of New York City, saw in his pastoral work how a housing situation contributes to human degradation. Health was impaired by negligence and the flaunting disregard of municipal regulations. Bribing of inspectors interfered with law enforcement.

He protested publicly and was threatened in an effort to intimidate him. He was discounted as "only a minister" having no competent knowledge of the problems of housing management. He was given "the runaround" and told to mind his own business. He persisted, however. Some newspapers and television stations helped him get public attention. The diocese of New York provided an able and conscientious lawyer, Mr. William Stringfellow, to help him put his evidence into proper form. Finally the city promised to undertake remedial steps.

The National Council of Churches has called attention to the human factors in the housing problem and has appeared before congressional hearings to present such testimony in connection with proposed legislation. Its staff officers co-operate with the Federal Housing Authority.

Lotteries and race-track betting are technical matters in relation to government income from taxation. The New York *World-Telegram and Sun*, on March 2, 1960, reported that Congressman Paul A. Fino had told the House of Representatives that a national lottery would give the government ten billion dollars a year in revenue. The churches have no special understanding of tax revenue production. Should they therefore say nothing about lotteries?

In addition to specific aspects of economic life, the purpose and the effects of economic systems involve moral values. Therefore, they should be kept constantly under scrutiny. There seems to be agreement among Christians that the churches should not identify any particular economic system with the Kingdom of God. On the contrary, existing systems must be kept under judgment in relation to the requirements of Christian standards. This does not mean that the churches should regard all systems as being equal in merit. There can be no question that the judgment against communism must in our day be much more severe than the judgment against capitalism.

The exploitation of natural resources is a moral as well as an economic problem. Waste of forests and minerals and careless farming which hastens soil erosion are sins against God and crimes against humanity. The Department of Agriculture appeals to the churches to arouse people's consciences.

One minister who preached against abuse of the soil and supported the government's recommendations for contour plowing and the planting of trees on marginal land was told by a man in his congregation that he owned his land and that no one had a right to tell him what he could do with it. He insisted that his costs of production were so high that he could not add to them any uneconomical expenses for the sake of the future. It was, he said, a matter of economics. But the community as a whole responded, and the protestor finally joined his neighbors in acting as a good steward of God's gifts.

The Competence of the Churches

While we distinguish between the technical and the moral aspects of economic life, we should remember that many of the professional experts in economics are members of churches. They share in formulating and adopting church policies and programs. They are aware of the limits of economic laws for determining economic life. They know also the importance of motives and purposes, of discipline and integrity in human relations as aspects of economic processes.

Moreover, the competence of some clergymen should not be too much discounted. They gain considerable insight into motives, values, and what economic life does to people. They learn much in the course of the pastoral counseling of individuals and families. They get close to people, to their hopes and fears, through discussions of the making of wills and disputes over them, through dealing with family tensions over income and expenditures and standards of living.

They see the consequences of poverty and unemployment. They observe the reactions to wealth among those who are habituated to it, those who have recently acquired it, those who have lost it, and those who are envious and ambitious to get it.

A minister can learn much about economic life from long hours spent with a man who, broken by financial ruin, struggles to adjust himself and finally yields to suicide. He also learns from such a man's family.

When the training and experience of informed laymen and clergy are combined under the discipline of moral responsibility in seeking the objectives to which the church is committed, they probably have a competence in analysis and evaluation of economic life at least equal to that of any other group in the community.

Even so, when the church deals with problems of economic life it should carefully distinguish between the factors on which it claims competence and responsibility and the technical factors. With regard to the latter, it should remind the specialists of their obligations to God and to society which should guide them in their work.

Rapid Social Change

In countries of Asia, Africa, and Latin America, industrialization has disrupted traditional social patterns, especially the tribal and family moral disciplines. As people move in great numbers from rural communities to cities, their whole way of life is upset. They often fall prey to evil influences. The changes which occurred gradually over several generations in Europe and America are abruptly introduced in the course of a couple of decades in some countries of Africa.

Various purposes have led to this development. The people in those countries have sought a higher standard of living. The technically advanced nations have wanted to help them. Some new enterprises have been stimulated by the desire for profitable capital investment from abroad. Moreover, prosperous countries offer new markets for export trade. Thus many Americans have an altruistic or a legitimate and even commendable economic interest in promoting such industrialization. But what is happening to the people in the process has not been anticipated or understood. Christians and others have become concerned.

A few years ago the World Council of Churches undertook a study of Christian Responsibility in Areas of Rapid Social Change in Asia, Africa, and Latin America. It was supported by a substantial grant of funds by the late John D. Rockefeller, Jr.

At an international conference in Greece in 1959, problems of nationalism, the Christian's responsibility in political life, and various cultural factors were discussed along with the economic aspects of social change. The relations of the West to these developments became quite apparent. The major emphasis, however, was on the dilemmas and opportunities for Christian action.

Already the churches in the lands most drastically affected by rapid social change and the missionary agencies are modifying their programs so as to be more helpful to people in new circumstances facing new temptations and new opportunities. The Gospel does not change, but the methods of evangelism and education as well as the programs of the churches and missions must be adapted to emerging situations.

Christian citizens in our country are becoming increasingly aware of the consequences of our national economic policies in the lives of millions overseas. Our foreign trade policy may undermine the economy of another people disastrously. A small change in our tariff on coffee can drastically affect Brazil.

The National Council of Churches and our denominational agencies are concerned about these matters and are informing the people in our churches so that they may act responsibly as Christian citizens. Through our close association with Christian leaders in other nations and our studies in co-operation with them, we are in a position to distinguish between sentimental gestures and real helpfulness. Christians have a special responsibility to challenge cheap, selfish propaganda about our government's policies.

The "Peaceful Atom"

We have at the same time been witnessing rapid social change in our own country. With it, new moral and ethical problems have been coming to light. The Department of the Church and Economic Life of the National Council of Churches and the denominational agencies have been alert. Some of the problems have technical aspects clearly beyond the competence of the churches. But the experts who deal with these aspects are usually eager to work with the churches to arouse Christian citizens to a concern for the human implications of technological developments.

The "peaceful atom" industry, for example, raises questions of moral responsibility. In one state alone there are 600 users of radioactive isotopes. Some twenty times within recent years crises have developed which threatened the health of whole communities. How can we induce people to think wisely about radiation hazards in their local situations?

How much risk should we accept in order to achieve progress? This is a question of concern to all the people. Only the scientists can tell us what the risks are; but values and lives are at stake, and the possible victims should share in the decisions. The situation is in some respects analogous to that in which a diseased person must rely on the doctor for diagnosis and an explanation of the risk involved and the chances of success in the proposed treatment by medicine or surgery. The patient or his family must make the basic decision as to whether to undergo the treatment, and frequently the minister is consulted.

A group of seventy-five scientists and church leaders, after analyzing their mutual involvement in significant new developments in the use of the atom, agreed that these questions should be on the conscience of church people, especially in our country, where the nuclear energy industry and the use of radioactive isotopes are developing so rapidly.

Automation

"Fourteen glass-blowing machines, operated by one worker, now produce 90 per cent of the glass light bulbs used in the United States and all the glass tubes used in radio and television sets (except picture tubes)." I find that statement difficult to believe but know and respect the source of it, David A. Morse, director general of the International Labor Organization, a specialized agency of the United Nations.

It has also been reported that in the United States automobile industry there are practically no non-automated plants for producing engines.

Such facts startle me. They are normal assumptions of today's generation of scientists and engineers, who are probably more concerned than I about the consequences of automation, because they understand better the implications of the machines and processes which they are developing.

W. H. Pickering of the California Institute of Technology, in the New York *Herald Tribune* of January 22, 1955, considers automation applied to military technology:

This is the prospect we face: the decision to destroy an enemy nation, and by inference our own, will be made by a radar set, a telephone circuit, an electronic computer. It will be arrived at without the aid of human intelligence. If a human observer cries: "Stop, let me check the calculations," he is already too late, his launching site is destroyed and the war is lost. . . .

This evolution from the push-button era to the automatic push-button era is inevitable. And when the day comes all the "human" considerations which might stay the hand of a warmonger will mean nothing.

Is there an answer? With the present political climate it is difficult to imagine what it could be. But if the answer is not found in a very few years, there will be no need for the answer because all that is left of humanity will be starting again the long climb from the stone age.

That seems almost fantastic. But it is in the field of science; and when the scientist talks in his own field, I am inclined to listen and to think. Perhaps he and I should spend more time discussing our mutual responsibilities. We would have little difficulty in defining and appreciating the respective roles of science and religion.

Leisure

Consider also some present and obvious consequences of automation and other technological development. There is nothing hypothetical about the increased productivity of man with his modern machine. There is already a margin of time and energy for the average man after he has done his job in production. What does he do with his leisure?

The September 1957 issue of *The Annals* of the American Academy of Political and Social Science contained twenty-seven articles on the general theme of "Recreation in the Age of Automation." The concluding paper contains this paragraph, which is perhaps not by intention a challenge to the churches:

The leisure mode, accompanied by many urgent problems, is taking its place in history. Its pattern stands in the line of evolution from feudalism, based on a stable agricultural society, through industrialism, based on a fruitful if strenuous factory system, to a creative and livable era characterized by freely disposable time and the wherewithal to enjoyment. The opportunity inherent in the promise is provided by the potent productive trinity—the scientist, the engineer, and the industrialist. The realization will depend upon the growth of man in spiritual stature, his competence for inner control, and his good sense and wisdom in pursuing values which his abundance enables him to possess.

It is encouraging to note that many churches, aware of the consequences of changes in economic life, are taking action by education and adjustments of parish programs to help people use leisure for constructive and creative purposes.

Wealth

While machines are freeing us from much routine drudgery, they are also conducive to mass organizations in industry and labor. Everything seems to be growing bigger and faster. But what about individuals? They are what really matter. The churches are concerned about what our wealth is doing to us or what we are doing with our wealth.

We Americans have been receiving higher and higher incomes. In spite of increasing living costs, we have a lot of money to spend. According to an Associated Press release, the Internal Revenue Service reported that the 1958 tax returns on income received in 1957 showed a record taxable income of $144,400,000,000. There were 59,825,000 returns, with

46,865,000 indicating taxable income—both new records. The total of individual income taxes, $34,400,000,000, was the biggest ever.

It is estimated that the United States, which has about 6 or 7 per cent of the world's population and 7 per cent of its area, turns out about 40 per cent of its production. In terms of industrial production, some estimates put our proportion higher.

A series of reports in the New York *World-Telegram and Sun* provided some interesting items of expenditure. In 1959 about 1.45 million United States citizens went abroad and spent about $2.3 billion. Those who took vacation trips at home spent $15.6 billion. A spokesman for the men's clothing industry said that men "no longer want just a suit, they want a certain look of elegance, smartness, and success." The National Cap and Cloth Hat Institute noted record sales. Advertising volume for all media approximated twelve billion dollars, up from ten billion in 1958. Bowling joined the nation's billion-dollar-a-year industries. Bowlers paid $440 million in bowling fees, and alley owners spent an additional $560 million for buildings and equipment.

Many new records are being established in wealth and material standards of living. Are we wiser? Are we happier? Are we more respected for the quality of our character as a people by the rest of mankind? These are questions the churches must ask.

Political Life

Our national tradition and constitutionally fixed policy of separation of church and state does not assume either that the government is indifferent or hostile to the interests of religion or that the church considers the government to be outside the realm of its concern. This is an important fact to keep in mind.

There were three principal reasons why the founders of our nation and those who adopted our Constitution insisted on the separation of church and state:

1. They believed in religious freedom. Therefore, on the basis of experience in the countries from which most of the colonists had come, they did not want one church to have the prestige, authority, and power of an established church, a position in which it might limit the rights of other churches.

2. They believed that the nation would be stronger if church and state were each free from control by the other. They knew of situations in which the state dominated the church, and others in which

the church controlled the state. Under those circumstances, neither could perform its functions freely and effectively.

3. They believed that religion thrives best when it relies upon the voluntary consent and loyalty of the believers. Religious commitment which is induced by the coercive power of the state backing up the church is neither significant nor reliable. So, they reasoned, the church is strongest when it stands on its own feet.

None of these reasons reflected antagonism to the church or to religion. None indicated an intention to discount the interests, values, or discipline of religion in the state, nor to eliminate the influence of the churches, taken together in their aggregate impact, from the processes of determining national policy.

The historical separation in some other countries has been for quite different reasons and reflects quite different national purposes. In the Soviet Union separation prevails, but the state is avowedly atheistic. It denies the values for which the church stands. The separation that prevails in France had its origins in a secularistic reaction against the church or in the rationalistic humanism of the French Revolution, of which the Goddess of Reason was the patron saint. That should be recognized as a contrast to the American principle, even though the patterns of separation are similar. Remember that our Declaration of Independence as originally drafted by Thomas Jefferson read, "All men are endowed with certain unalienable rights," and that it was amended by the Congress to read, "All men are endowed by their Creator with certain unalienable rights."

The important point is that the ground and purpose of separation was for us by no means secularistic, whereas for some others it has been. Consequently the church and the values for which it stands are appropriately assumed to be factors of influence in the national life in relation to government and political life.

It follows that the church is not expected to be a subservient or involuntary instrument of the policy and program of the national government. At the same time, it may appropriately support the government's policy and program when they are consonant with the principles of the church.

The State Is Not Morally Autonomous

One of the most important functions of the church is to remind the state that it is not a law unto itself, that it is not morally autonomous, that it subsists under the governance of God and is therefore to be judged by His laws. "The powers that be are ordained of God"; but that does not mean that they can do whatever they like to serve their own ends or to disregard the rights of other peoples who are also a part of God's creation and concern.

This is a matter of special importance today, for the role of government has become enlarged. Modern interdependent mass society, with its large concentrations of economic power affecting the lives of all citizens, requires strong and extensive operations and controls by a central governmental authority in the interest of the entire citizenship. Moreover, the problem of the security and independence of a people in the present world situation imposes upon the government of a nation a responsibility that calls for the mobilization of all resources under one effective co-ordinating direction.

A national government is therefore tempted to assume that it has all power and absolute sovereignty. When it does so, and asks the people to concede it such prerogatives, it leads the people to idolatry of the state. Then the witness of the church becomes most difficult and most necessary, for it must call the state to account before the moral law of the Sovereign God who rules in history over all nations.

One of the most important actions of the churches in recent years was a statement by the General Board of the National Council of Churches on March 17, 1954, in that era when the phenomenon known as "McCarthyism" was threatening to put certain instruments of the national government above the rule of law and the established procedures of justice. In several instances it had succeeded and won the support of some powerful elements in the nation. It had exploited a really grave situation in such a way as to increase fear and panic. Many people were willing to surrender democratic rights and processes. Opposition was not popular.

The National Council of Churches, noting the danger, set up a Committee on the Maintenance of American Freedom, under the chairmanship of the Right Rev. Henry Knox Sherrill, presiding bishop of the Protestant Episcopal Church and a former president of the National Council. This committee, after a careful study, recommended that the General Board analyze and challenge the menacing trend in our national life. It submitted a draft of a historical statement.

The statement criticized procedural abuses by certain congressional committees. This protest was necessary and practical. But the heart of the matter was in the following paragraph:

A more basic threat has been a growing tendency on the part of our people and their representatives in government to suppose that it is within the competence of the state to determine what is and what is not American. The American way is to preserve freedom by encouraging diversity within the unity of the nation and by trusting truth to prevail over error in open discussion. The American way is to depend upon the educational institutions to seek the truth and teach it without fear. The American way is to look to the churches in the richness of their diversity to bring to the nation light and discipline from God to maintain a responsible freedom.

The General Board, with only two negative votes recorded, adopted the statement. Similar actions by member churches confirmed the judgment of their delegates to the General Board that this was what the churches should say to the nation in a time of crisis. The public and leaders in government took notice. Some magazines in other nations credited our churches with the decisive influence on the side of reason and freedom in a situation of crisis in our national life.

The statement was not directed specifically to government. It had its effect directly upon Christian citizens and ultimately upon government.

The Christian Citizen in Political Life

It can be seen in this instance and in general that political life is broader and more fundamental than government, at least in our democracy. The Christian citizen is a voter, but he is also a unit of influence and decision in determining the national trend.

In our political system, the rank-and-file citizens do, in the long run, have an effective voice. What happens at the ward level is important, and it is at that level where the average citizen should start his work. That is the "grass roots" of political life.

The churches are encouraging their members to become active in political life, beginning at the local community level. Many of our "better" people hesitate to become involved in "politics." It is a sad and alarming commentary on our national life that politics has come to be regarded by many as a somewhat disreputable field of activity. To be sure, it is in some places a rather rough activity. I remember a conversation with a good church member who wanted to discuss with me whether he should run for an elective office. He was concerned about many matters of public policy. His associates told him that he should be willing to battle for his ideas in the arena of public political contest. He shrank from that. But some of his friends jibed that he was "afraid to get his feet muddy" in politics. That troubled him. I agreed that he would probably be hurt. He ran and lost, but he kept at it and became a most useful public servant.

Instead of disdaining the field of political life, the churches are encouraging responsible Christian citizens to seek elective office or to enter government service in an executive capacity, even if it entails a loss of income and the disruption of an orderly and comfortable life. Moreover, it sometimes involves a sacrifice on the part of his family.

When a church member as a matter of Christian vocation enters actively into political life, he should have continuing pastoral help. But it does not follow that the church should seek votes for him or other support unless he has superior competence in comparison with his rivals or unless the policies he advocates are sound.

The responsible Christian citizen votes not only for "the man" but also for the candidate's policies and for the party with which he is affiliated. Personal integrity is important, but it is not enough, so the avowed and articulate churchman should not expect or receive the support of his fellow church members unless his policies and performance merit such support. The important point here is that the church encourages responsible and competent Christian citizens to enter public service in the field of political life.

The Churches' Role of Analysis

In addition, the churches, in their corporate life as institutions in the local, state, or national communities, have a responsibility in political life, first to their members, second to the public, and third to the instrumentalities of government.

The church owes it to its members to help them, working together under the aegis of the church, to define the moral and ethical standards by which to judge issues and to evaluate men in, or seeking, public office. To do so is not to make up their minds for them but to help them achieve the perspective and the criteria for sound decisions. The choices lie with their own individual insights and consciences; but guiding principles, which they themselves clarify, are not often apparent in general public debate.

Supplementary to such basic study is the analysis or evaluation of the propaganda promoted by partisan pressure groups and agencies and most of the mass media of communication. Special-interest groups are seldom labeled as such, and if they are "uncovered" or "exposed" it is often by a rival special-interest group. The average thoughtful citizen tends to accept as authority the organization or newspaper or commentator which seems to support his own interest.

If the church fulfills its responsibility of objectivity and fairness, it renders great service by impartial investigation of the interests and purposes motivating the selection and interpretation of the news in its bearing on political issues. On the basis of repeated experiments in discussing the church and public affairs with church groups I have found it instructive to compare various reports of the same events.

I take one illustration: An important political event had occurred in London the day before a group met in a New York church. Members of the group gave varying and, at some points, contradictory reports. When challenged as to their sources of information, most cited newspapers or commentators; a few had picked up impressions from overheard conversations; one had read a headline over the shoulder of a fellow subway passenger and had drawn his own conclusions.

I produced five different newspapers with stories of the event. Three of them were based on the same syndicated report, but by their selection of certain items and not others they gave different emphases and impressions. The headlines, which induce an initial mindset in the reader, varied considerably. The three papers conveyed three different understandings, though they had the same source before them. The other two papers gave different interpretations based on their own correspondents' observations.

The group were surprised and annoyed. Some were indignant. They began to discuss why there were such differences. This was the important question. They described the "lines" of the different papers and the interests they served more or less obviously. Then they discussed what they thought was really important in the London event.

Thus they became more responsible citizens, with some common-sense appraisals and some guiding Christian principles which they formulated largely by themselves, under the encouragement and the aegis of the church.

Ministers and other church leaders often know more than the general public about the purposes and methods of propaganda agencies. It would be amusing, if it were not so disgusting, to list the methods by which ministers are cultivated, solicited, and threatened in order to induce them to oppose or endorse a cause or organization, or just to keep quiet. They often know what organizations or magazines or broadcast programs are subsidized by whom and for what purposes.

One way to know about such matters is to compare the reporter's account of an event with the account published in his magazine. When the editor twists and distorts his own reporter's story, it is easy to discover the "line" or "pitch" the magazine wants to "put over."

I do not want to give the impression that all organizations and all mass-media agencies are irresponsible. They are not. And those that are outspokenly partisan are more to be trusted than those that try to give the impression of being non-partisan but are not. Fortunately there are many agencies—partisan and non-partisan—which effectively serve the public interest without deviating from moral or professional integrity.

One of the important functions of the churches concerning public affairs—especially political and economic life—is to help Christian citizens become informed and discriminating in their choice of the authorities on which they rely.

Among the most useful services of councils of churches is that of keeping the churches informed of impending decisions by legislative bodies or executive agencies on matters of special concern to church people. The "Washington Office Reports" of the National Council of Churches provide information to the member denominations on a list of subjects which the denominations themselves provide. The reports give the main features of bills, the influences for and against, and where they stand in the legislative process. They do not tell people what position they should take.

State and local councils provide similar services at their respective levels of governmental and political operations.

Freedom and Order

One of the problems of political life in a democracy is to maintain a proper balance between freedom and order. Traditionally we Americans have emphasized freedom—"the less government the better." We have engaged in endless debate over the respective roles of the federal and state governments. In time of national crisis we enlarge the functions of the federal government in the interest of order, the general welfare, and national security.

We generally believe it to be unwise for people to rely on government to solve all our problems. Character develops through self-reliance. On the other hand, in contemporary mass society, with mechanization in industry destroying the market for many skills responsibly developed yesterday, the individual may be helpless if left to his own initiative, especially if he is a city dweller. Then we ask government action in the interest of justice and order.

Moreover, with the growth of powerful organizations in economic life, strong government is needed when these organizations get into a deadlock of conflict. There is a limit as to how long a steel strike can be permitted to continue; the nation as a whole has some rights to welfare and security.

So the tendency is to bigger government and to increased centralization of control. The alternative, or the check, is voluntary co-ordination and discipline of citizens and decentralized groups.

Here the churches, by loyalty to their beliefs and demonstration in their life and structure, make an impact on political life. The Protestant doctrine of the mutual priesthood of believers and their direct accountability to God provides the basis for both voluntarism and discipline, which make freedom safe and workable in society, including political life.

Professor John T. McMill says, in *Foundations of Democracy:*

The Reformation doctrine of the priesthood of all Christians . . . has been widely misinterpreted. . . . It is glibly made the equivalent of a mere naked individualism in which every Christian is his own priest; and it is alleged to abolish priesthood itself. In fact, it extends priestly functions to all true Christians and makes every Christian his neighbor's priest. "By that priesthood," says Luther, in a typical statement, "we are able to appear before God, to pray for others, and to teach one another mutually the things that are of God". . . . The whole conception is of fellowship arising in the religious sphere and extending to social and economic mutual service.

The forms and processes of American political life were derived in large measure from the Protestant churches. Chief Justice Tilghman wrote: "The forms of the Constitution of the United States borrowed very much of the forms of our Republic from the Constitution of the Presbyterian Church of Scotland."

Looking broadly at the western world, the eminent sociologist, Carl Mannheim, in his book *Diagnosis of Our Time,* says: "The genuine contribution of Protestantism is bound to come from its emphasis on voluntary co-operation, self-help and mutual aid. These will always be the great antitheses to the coming forms of authoritarianism, centralization and organization from above."

Our councils of churches demonstrate by structure, procedure, and program operations how to keep freedom and order in balance. The member churches maintain their freedom and autonomy. At the same time, they voluntarily co-ordinate their interest when, as, and if they choose, thus achieving order and avoiding frustrating fragmentation.

The major Protestant churches in this country are frequently engaged in discussion and modification of their organizations, moving toward centralization, then toward decentralization, and then back to where they were before. To some this may seem wasteful and frustrating. In my judgment it is an indication of creative vitality.

Thus, in the councils of churches and in the several denominations, Protestants continue by teaching and demonstration to make their historic contribution to American political life at the point of one of its most perplexing quandaries.

Morality and Ethical Standards

Remembering that we are concerned in this book with the churches and public affairs, we shall deal only with a few illustrations of morality and ethical standards of conduct as they become matters of public responsibility.

Unlike economic life and politics, few responsible citizens question the need for improvement or the appropriateness of the churches' intervention. It is obvious that morals and ethics in the individual's private conduct and in interpersonal relations are the business of the church, at least in teaching.

Even when these matters get into the public domain and public regulations and discipline become necessary, it is generally admitted that the church should normally become involved. When it comes to the point of legislation, the debate begins as to what and how much should be done and whether the church knows what it is talking about. Then it is pointed out, with some slight justification, that the church confesses failure when it seems to rely on law to correct evils and abuses that should be prevented by the development of character and discipline in individual people.

Public opinion, the prevailing popular standards of conduct, and the "conscience of the people" are relevant, along with the teaching of the church among its members. Thus the church, as an institution in the community, must exert its influence publicly.

Integrity in Public Agencies

Consider the problem of integrity in the service of government. Under different administrations in Washington there have been people who have accepted personal profit or advantage because of their positions of influence or authority. Embarrassment has arisen in connection with vicuña coats, deep-freezers, oriental rugs, holidays at expensive hotels, unexplained income from drug companies.

"Payola" is a recently coined word in the broadcasting industry to describe a practice, not an isolated instance. "Fixed" quiz programs became a shocking scandal, almost forgotten after a few months. Some drug advertising has been officially condemned as misleading. Officers have used labor-union funds for personal purposes. Meat-store scales have been adjusted to cheat the customers, and inspectors have been bribed. Theses are bought for submission for academic degrees and substitutes hired by students to take their examinations for them.

The reader can add a list of corruptions from his own reading and knowledge. The most alarming feature of the problem is the mildness of the shock that people register when they learn about shady and illegal practices. Many comment: "It's done everywhere. He just got caught." It is the low standard of expectancy that is the worst problem.

Gambling

Getting something for nothing at other people's expense is morally poisonous, whether in business, politics, or gambling.

The New York *Times* of January 14, 1960, reported that legalized bingo games and raffles in New Jersey grossed $30,825,606 in 1959, which was $2,401,837 more than in 1958.

The amount of money involved in such games is trifling in comparison with betting on horse races. As a pastor, I had seen its ruinous consequences in the lives of individuals and families. But I had not given it much attention until I had a shock at its extent.

One day in 1945 I read that a crowd of 49,614 at Belmont Park established a world-record betting total of $5,016,745 as well as a world mark for daily-double wagering. The figure of five million plus was arresting to me because earlier that day the representatives of most of the major Protestant churches of our country had been considering whether we would be able to raise five million dollars for the churches' relief program in Europe for that desperate winter right after the war. Our conclusion had been: Probably not.

My arithmetic showed that the average amount wagered by each person at Belmont Park that Saturday afternoon had been about $101.12. (And the dollar was worth more then.) In addition to that amount, I assumed that it cost something to get to Belmont and something for admission. I did not pretend to understand the ways of betting people, but I assume that they might have given $5,016,745 to relief without sacrificing to the point of hardship.

The total revenue to the New York State Treasury from thorough-

bred racing in 1959 was $51,533,924, according to the annual report
of the State Racing Commission, reviewed in the New York *Times*
of January 12, 1960. The average daily bet per person was $95.28.
The state's income was a record, thanks to the addition of a new
track at Aqueduct, where 1,847,592 persons wagered $178,095,629.

On July 5, 1960 the *Times* reported that on July 4 at the Aqueduct
track 57,141 fans wagered $4,406,345, "the eighth highest handle in
New York racing." (The attendance had been 70,992 on Memorial
Day.) According to the same paper, $2,264,905 was the "mutual han-
dle" at Arlington Park, a Chicago track. I wish I knew what the total
was for all the tracks in the country for that one day.

The General Board of the National Council of Churches on March
26, 1951, adopted a resolution from which I take the following:

Gambling has become a commercial enterprise on a national scale. It
is also becoming clear that there is a connection between organized gambling and crime. We affirm again our vigorous opposition to gambling
as an insidious menace both to personal character and social morality.

The social malady of gambling will not be remedied by criminal
prosecutions alone. Stricter standards of moral integrity must be cultivated
in the community as a whole. Government, the press, public education
and all other civic agencies have a responsibility for this. But the churches
have a special duty. The strengthening of moral fibre is one of their pre-
eminent tasks.

The so-called "innocent" forms of gambling—such as legalized race-
track wagers, betting on athletic events, lotteries, bingo, and the like—
contribute to the weakening of the moral fibre of the individual and lower
the moral tone of the community.

The state legislatures and the local police and courts are strategic in
the battle for public policy and control. State and local councils of
churches do their best, but sometimes they have only indifferent support. To some extent, support is undermined by prominent religious
leaders who de-emphasize the importance of such problems of morals
and ethics.

Some theologians, I believe, have gone farther in discounting "mor-
alism" than has been wise or necessary. I agree that the influence of
the churches must be effective at the centers of the power structures
of our day and at the points where crucial immediate decisions are
made. "Summit" conferences, appropriations for technical assistance,
national elections are crucial. But the national character and our
standards and patterns of conduct as a people are just as potent factors

of influence in determining the line-up of the peoples of the world as our missiles and our budget for defense. A nation in which so many people live by the standard of "whether you can get away with it," and blame is assigned for being caught, gets into real trouble in the power struggle of international relations through its behavior in a U-2 incident.

Highway Murder

Another problem to which church people are too indifferent is highway deaths. Over the Independence Day weekend of 1960, it was reported that 442 people were killed in accidents on the roads. This was a record. The National Safety Council had made an advance estimate of 370. It characterized the actual toll as "appalling."

Some of these accidents were due to mechanical failures, but most were caused by human failure. There are inevitable hazards of miscalculation or inadequate skill, some of which can be reduced by diligent attention and caution. But it is the human failures that result from a lack of discipline which should concern church people most.

The breakdown of discipline results, I believe, from a deterioration of respect for the value of human life, a low sense of responsibility for other people's lives, even for one's own. Reduced to its simplest terms, the human failure goes back to an attitude which in effect is this: "I want what I want, now! And if somebody gets hurt, well, it's too bad." That person lacks both self-respect and a decent regard for other human beings. He is a menace to himself, to his neighbors, and to society. And if he is on the highway, especially if he has been drinking, someone is going to get hurt, if not killed.

A man's car is his private property, but when he is in it on a highway he is in the public domain and is no longer a private citizen. When he takes hold of the steering wheel he is no longer free to follow his own impulses. Whether he drinks or not before driving is not his free choice; it is society's.

Preventable highway deaths are a serious matter, but they are a symptom of a grave national problem; for when life is regarded as cheap, society is in a bad way. Our society has been marked traditionally by its high regard for the value of the human being. And this evaluation has derived in large measure from a religious concept of man. Consequently, any cheapening of life is a challenge to the religious forces of the nation.

I cannot understand why the churches have not been more con-

cerned about this problem. Perhaps they think accidents are just bad
luck. Perhaps they think it is only a problem of law enforcement; if
so, they have not thought twice.

Some church people are concerned. In September 1959, I participated in a conference at North Conway, New Hampshire, which should
be copied in general form and substance in every state. It was spon-
sored by the North Conway Foundation, which is led by churchmen
concerned about the problem of alcoholism. Any state council of
churches could do the same thing.

The theme of the conference was "Drinking Drivers and Drunken
Pedestrians." Participating organizations included the Executive De-
partment of New Hampshire, the Attorney General's Office, and the
state departments of Motor Vehicles, Education and Public Welfare,
the State Police, the New Hampshire Police Chief's Association, the
University of New Hampshire, the New Hampshire Citizen's Traffic
Safety Council, the New Hampshire Christian Civic League, and the
New Hampshire Council of Churches.

This mobilization of resources, with churchmen in the lead, shows
what can be done when a few people go into action. Various community agencies are now aroused and co-operating.

Youth Reflects Our Culture

What we usually call "juvenile delinquency" is another alarming
symptom of the chaos in morality and the ethical standards of conduct in our culture. The obvious manifestations in gang warfare and
other forms of violence are well known, and the churches are giving
them attention in programs both preventive and remedial. I would
make only one point here to suggest the depth of the problem.

Youth today is milling around in the turmoil of a hectic world of
change and confused standards without a sense of direction. We may
be grateful that they are restless and at loose ends. It would be more
alarming if they were complacent, tame, and dull. Their worst enemies
are cynicism and nihilism, which are not their creation but the enemies
which we of the older generation have inadvertently brought into our
society to fill the vacuum resulting from our lack of clearly defined
ideals and purposes.

The "beatniks" and "drugstore cowboys"—to be distinguished from
the lawless element—will become orderly, creative, and disciplined in
their own way if we help them find significant, exciting, and absorbing
goals and purposes.

Social Welfare

The average Christian citizen is perplexed about how to fulfill his responsibilities to his fellow men and to the community through social welfare services. There are so many "worthy causes" to support, so many demands on his budget.

First there are taxes, not only the big federal income tax and for some a state income tax, but also real estate, sales, excise, travel, amusements, luxuries, car, and other taxes. These provide, in addition to public services from which he obviously benefits (police and fire protection, roads, national defense, etc.), a number of public welfare services from which others may benefit more than he. He may also make a social security payment either as employer or as employee. Some of his tax money goes for assistance to the people of underdeveloped countries.

Second come the Community Chest and an endless parade of solicitors at the door and letters appealing for all sorts of reputable health foundations, children's homes and camps, hospitals, the Red Cross, Alma Mater, and service-club projects which are not included in the Chest.

Third comes the church, with its budget including current operating expenses, foreign and home missions, the parish educational program, denominational seminaries and colleges, and the church appeal for overseas relief and reconstruction, the denominational welfare institutions, and the local community welfare services of the church.

Fourth, he has personal obligations to help an aged or infirm relation or someone else in special trouble.

He sees good and obvious reasons for most of these and wants to do his rightful part. But he really wonders why—with the government and so many other good agencies in the same field—the church also has to have welfare institutions and a parish social welfare program.

He has no choice about the taxes, and he may have no complaint about them, recognizing them as sound social policy, though he probably grumbles occasionally along with his neighbors. He assumes that government provides for most of the essential needs of people. He hears on every side that we are in the era of the "welfare state."

Perhaps he thinks the present system is better than the old. Perhaps he does not. But he accepts it and is paying for it. He may or may not feel that the designation "welfare state" has a damning connotation, as it has for many Americans, that it has been usually used in public debate as an expletive to arouse emotion rather than as an objective definition. No matter what his judgment, the concept has got into his consciousness as denoting a significant change in the role of government.

He realizes, of course, that the government cannot and should not do everything for people in trouble. But what need is left over, he reasons, can be met by the well-established voluntary agencies in and beyond the Community Chest without the help of the church. Moreover, the church has all it can do to meet the costs of its own special religious work, education, and missions that no one else can do. Why, then, does it really have to be in the social welfare field when there are others to take care of it?

Admittedly, the church at an earlier stage in history was the primary welfare agency. It pioneered. Then its influence for justice was so effective that the whole community recognized its responsibilities and has taken it over.

No wonder the man in the pew is perplexed. As he considers his benevolence budget, he faces many of the policy problems of the church and the state in their respective roles in modern society. He may be driven to distraction trying to distinguish between what is secular and what is Christian.

The churches themselves were for many years without a clear social welfare policy. Some of them, finding it difficult to maintain financial support, discontinued building new institutions and turned many hospitals and homes over to cities or to non-sectarian boards. Others continued to expand their programs. The different actions reflected, in general, different traditions.

A brief review of recent national history may help the conscientious but perplexed church member. The welfare services required during the depression of the 1930's were beyond the total capacities of all the private agencies. Additional community-wide campaigns for relief funds were insufficient. Government stepped in. Whether it did so of its own free choice or inescapable necessity was and is a matter of debate. But we should not forget the veterans' march on Washington and the sporadic outbreaks of disorder by the unemployed. Normal economic measures and community patterns of social welfare service had broken down. The demand for government intervention was widespread.

The war came next, with a greatly enlarged role for government. It urged voluntary self-restraint against hoarding, but soon there was a demand for rationing in the interest of justice and equity. The government regulated most aspects of public life.

For nearly two decades, through two succeeding periods of crisis, the relative responsibilities of government agencies and private agencies were drastically changed—almost reversed—from the traditional balance. Government became clearly predominent.

The trend had begun earlier, however. It should not be attributed to one political party or administration. President Hoover's Research Commission on Social Trends had said in its 1932 report: "The shifting of economic activities had brought innumerable problems to the government. It has forced an expansion of governmental functions, creating problems of bureaucracy and inefficiency." That was before the days of the New Deal.

After the war it was clear that the churches and the non-sectarian private welfare agencies had been squeezed into a narrower sector of function and responsibility in the community pattern. And the community chests and unaffiliated agencies were crowding the churches in competition for voluntary contributions. The churches found themselves without clear policy as to their role in social welfare.

They decided to undertake a basic and comprehensive study of their position. Through the Department of Social Welfare of the National Council of Churches they undertook three years of exploration and research and held seventy-five conferences from coast to coast to appraise their resources and programs in preparation for the first National Conference on the Church and Social Welfare at Cleveland in November 1955. Denominations and councils of churches sent fifteen hundred delegates.

As a result of the studies and the conference, the churches got a clear picture of the total social welfare situation in the nation, the aggregate institutional resources of the churches, the types of services they were providing, the costs of operation, and the sources of income. But they also came to realize that well-tabulated information did not provide answers to their most important questions and that they needed a clearer understanding of the nature of the church and its role in society, based on biblical and theological grounds.

The Department of Social Welfare then polled two thousand church and welfare leaders to discover the precise questions of basic policy and purpose that had to be answered before a decision could be reached on what the churches should do. Historians and theologians went to work along with the sociologists.

Denominations and state and local councils of churches sent 265 selected leaders as delegates to a National Conference on Policy and Strategy in Social Welfare at Atlantic City in May 1957. That conference produced a report to the churches which was at once recognized by them as providing a clarification of role and a sense of direction.

Thus, during the period from 1952 to 1957, the churches found out where they were in the social welfare scene and arrived at a substantial measure of agreement on where they ought to be and why. The man in the pew does not yet realize that these developments have taken place. This brief review, presented out of sympathy with his perplexity, is intended to give him confidence that the churches now know what they are doing and why.

The Churches' Whole Witness

He should read and examine for himself, however, some of the assumptions underlying the church programs he is asked to support. The basic reasons the churches cannot leave social welfare services entirely to the government and private secular agencies are set forth in these excerpts from the Atlantic City conference report:

Social welfare is an integral part of the ministry of the church, not an optional part of its program. As God reveals himself in Jesus Christ, this involvement in the totality of man's life becomes evident. In order for the Church to be true to its role as the Body of Christ, it must manifest Christ's concern and compassionate action wherever there is human need. In response to the grace of God, the Church is impelled to awaken and maintain among its members awareness of, sensitivity to, and creativity in serving the whole man in all his relationships, and all men as children of God. Even though it exists under judgment, this world is a real province of the kingdom of God; thus a concern for spiritual realities involves activity in the total life of man. Various formulations can be given to the basic motivation of church and Christian to engage in social welfare. It is done out of gratitude in response to God's act in Jesus Christ as an expression of faith. It is done under the impulsion of the Holy Spirit as a response to our neighbor's needs. It is done as an essential part of our Christian witness. All of these point to the fact that the social welfare activity of the Church is inherent in its primary mission. It is another part of its proclamation of the gospel. The various aspects of this proclamation are so interrelated that to isolate or ignore any of them is dangerous to the fundamental purpose of the Church. . . .

It seems clear in the New Testament that the task of the Church involves three central aspects. First, there is the impartation of the gospel (kerygma), which includes the spoken word, the preaching and teaching of the 'good news' of the incarnation, death and resurrection of Jesus Christ; secondly, there is the fellowship of participation together (koinonia) in the encounter of Jesus Christ with the world; and thirdly, the expression of the Christian faith in love and service to all men (diakonia). . . .

The Church is constrained to give expression to all three aspects of its mission in every generation in order to declare the continuation of the acts of God, supremely revealed and expressed in the life, death, and resurrection of Jesus Christ. All three aspects are related to the Kingdom which has come and is coming.

Our churches have been formulating policy, not only in the light of theology and the analysis of history in this country, but also on the basis of observing what has happened in other nations. Some of our friends in Germany have vivid memories of a time when the state became so all-embracing as to be regarded as synonymous with the community. That situation is also the objective of communism in countries where it is in control today. People are taught to think of social welfare in physical, biological, and psychological terms and tend to become that kind of being.

Moreover, in the communist society the state is interested first and foremost in industry, so we see in extreme form the problem of personality in the age of technology. For the communist believes that technics can be applied to community life and to the relation of the person to the community.

In such societies the churches are forced into detachment from the community. When that happens, their witness becomes partial and therefore distorted.

We believe that all men need a sense of being related to God and to a community. The church is the most meaningful, healing, and restoring community. Men in need of welfare services need the church in its totality.

Voluntary organizations, especially church agencies—even if their scope is limited—are essential in a free society also as a means of avoiding state monopoly and of encouraging individual growth in responsibility.

There are some types of need in which the total ministry of the church is especially important; unmarried mothers, for example. Material and spiritual aid should go together.

There are, then, two guiding principles of fundamental policy which put the churches under orders in providing a ministry of social welfare: (1) Man's need is not only physical and psychological, but also moral and spiritual. "Man does not live by bread alone." (2) The church must render service in the name of Christ to the whole man to be true to its own nature and function.

Church Welfare Institutions

A few health and welfare service estimates, compiled by Dr. Charles G. Chakerian and Dr. William J. Villaume and based upon research, provide a rough idea of the program of the denominations and its relation to the total national program. It should be remembered that these figures do not include local parish services.

In 1953 the national health and welfare bill was $20,000,000,000. Of this, $16,000,000,000 was provided by local, state, and federal governments, $1,700,000,000 by private non-sectarian sources, and $2,300,-000,000 by all church sources.

In 1954 about 4,000 Protestant and Eastern Orthodox health and welfare agencies and institutions served 17,000,000 persons, of whom about 35 per cent were not of the Protestant or Eastern Orthodox faiths. Serving these agencies and institutions were 200,000 full-time personnel, 155,000 volunteers, and 70,000 board members. They employed about 26,000 medical doctors, 37,500 registered nurses, 14,400 social workers, and 25,000 other professional people.

Their capital assets were about $3,350,000,000, of which 53.8 per cent was in buildings, land, and equipment, and 46.2 in endowments and investments. Sixty per cent of the institutions had been established before 1930.

Among the 4,000 Protestant and Eastern Orthodox agencies and institutions, there were 700 homes for the aged (about 24 per cent of all public and private homes for the aged), 800 providing services to children, 600 hospitals, 550 neighborhood houses and settlements, 120 family welfare agencies, 170 camps, 475 residences, hospices, and temporary shelters.

In general, the denominations have been increasing their programs during the last several years. For example, the Board of Hospitals and Homes of the Methodist Church reports that the number of its affiliated institutions increased from 229 in 1958 to 236 in 1959. Increases occurred also in the total capacity of institutions, doctors on staff, assets, operating costs, and income from churches.

I have given considerable emphasis to the basic questions about which I think there is most perplexity and confusion in the minds of thoughtful Christian citizens. I have also given some facts about church institutions. But I do not want to leave the impression that the churches have been giving all their attention to defining policies and maintaining institutions.

Church Influence on National Policy

While doing these things the churches have also been fulfilling their responsibility to influence national policies. They have reminded the American people of the demands of social justice by testifying to the concerns of Christian conscience in connection with measures before Congress and by working closely with the executive branch of government in order to keep the concerns of the churches constantly before them.

The National Council of Churches has adopted and distributed carefully prepared statements on the churches' concern for housing and for health services, and pronouncements on alcohol, gambling, and public morals.

The Department of Social Welfare, on behalf of the constituent churches, has maintained a close relationship with many agencies, conferences, and councils of the federal government, including the White House Conference on Children and Youth, the White House Conference on Aging, the Conference on Homemakers Services, the Advisory Council on Child Welfare Services, the President's Committee on Youth Fitness, the Housing and Home Finance Agency, the Bureau of Public Assistance, the Bureau of Old Age and Survivors' Insurance, the President's Committee on Employment of the Physically Handicapped, and others.

By keeping close to the many ramifications of the government's program in social welfare, the churches can support the extension of services in the areas of greatest need, influence the depth and quality of the services, and also help to keep the program from presumptuous purposes and monopoly.

State and local councils of churches enable their constituents to maintain the same kind of influence at their respective levels of government.

I would also reiterate the great importance of the social welfare program of the local church (see Chapter II). It is, of course, of greater total effect than all the denominations' social welfare institutions put together. The considerations that I have reviewed with regard to the role of the churches nationally are relevant, at most points, to the parish and the local community.

In my opinion, the study of the role of the churches in social welfare in the world, the nation, the state, and the local community is the most normal, basic, and productive way for a denomination or a local church to find its proper place in public affairs. Such study obviously requires analyses of our social situation, contemporary culture, the modern state, and the nature and mission of the church.

I make a special urgent plea to the churches: Do not consider social welfare a "cause" that can be left to those who have a special interest in it. What you decide to do about it determines to a considerable extent what you can do about contemporary society, about race relations, and about international relations. For it is at this point especially that you will decide what you think a Christian church is in terms of action in the world.

Communism

The churches should have their own case against communism and their own policy and strategy for dealing with it, even though there are many points at which they may appropriately support government policies. Communism is a philosophy as well as a social, political, and economic program. As a philosophy, it is antithetical to Christianity. As a program, it is hostile to the church and its influence. Therefore, the churches should not be content merely to endorse government programs and to add their sanction to popular opinion.

The official communist line against religion and the party's strategy for dealing with the churches in the Soviet Union were set forth most fully in a decree of the party's Central Committee, signed by N. Khrushchev and published in *Pravda*, November 11, 1954. That line is characteristic of communist philosophy everywhere. But the strategy is quite different from that which prevails in some, if not most, of the other communist-controlled countries.

After thirty-seven years of persecution and abuse, largely liquidating the churches' leadership and almost wrecking their organization, the party found that religious beliefs persisted and that churches were supporting much of the communist social, political, and economic program that seemed to them to be in the interest of human justice and the national welfare. So the party adopted a subtle and sophisticated policy based on the conclusion that it was futile to make martyrs of believers and psychologically unwise to concede to them the strength and importance implied in showing fear of them.

Anti-Religious Strategy

The new strategy amounts to this: Step up the campaign of scientific atheistic education. Treat the believers with confident nonchalance, then religion will disappear with the dying generation. Do not interfere with the internal life of the churches so long as they do nothing inimical to the social, political, and economic program of the party. Challenge only the religious philosophy which is represented among the remnant of believers.

This strategy is probably more difficult for the churches to meet than the former persecution.

In the party's own language, the case may be seen in the following quotations from its decree:

The fundamental opposition of science and religion is obvious. Whereas science relies on facts, scientific experiment and conclusions strictly checked and confirmed by life, any religion bases itself only on biblical and other traditions, on fantastic fabrications. Modern scientific discoveries in the natural and social sciences convincingly refute religious dogmas. . . .

As a result of profound changes in the social-economic conditions of life, the liquidation of exploiter classes and the victory of socialism in the U.S.S.R., as a result of the successful development of science and the general rise in the level of culture in the country, the majority of the population of the Soviet Union has long been freed of religious survivals; the consciousness of the working people has grown immeasurably. At the same time, one cannot but take into account the fact that there are also many citizens who, while actively participating in the life of the country and honorably fulfilling their civic duty to the motherland, are still under the influence of various kinds of religious beliefs. The Party has always demanded and will continue to demand a considerate, mindful attitude toward these believers. All the more is it stupid and harmful to cast political doubt on Soviet citizens because of their religious convictions. Profound, patient, skillfully arranged scientific-atheist propaganda among believers will help them in the long run to free themselves from religious delusions. On the other hand, administrative [i.e., penalizing—Translator] measures of any kind and insulting attacks on believers and clergy can only do harm, can only lead to strengthening and even intensifying their religious convictions. . . .

Therefore, the struggle against religious beliefs should be regarded now as an ideological struggle of the scientific, materialist world outlook against an anti-scientific, religious world outlook.

Rectification of mistakes committed in anti-religious propaganda must not lead to relaxation of scientific-atheistic propaganda, which is an integral part of the communist education of the working people and has as its aim the dissemination of scientific, materialistic knowledge among the masses and the liberation of believers from the influence of religious beliefs. . . .

The Party Central Committee emphasizes that scientific-atheistic propaganda requires the greatest care and thought in the selection of lecturers, speakers and authors of articles and pamphlets on anti-religious subjects.

In the East Zone of Germany, where the communists did not establish their rule until 1946, and where there are strong churches, the propaganda is the same in substance, but the strategy with regard to the churches is different. First, the government tried to nationalize East German Protestantism (about 90 per cent of the church-going population) and set up a group of "active peace pastors," but only half of one per cent joined. Next they tried starving the churches financially.

Conflict flared into the open in 1949 with the reading of a pastoral letter from Bishop Otto Dibelius in the pulpits of the churches, in which he protested against "force which goes beyond all rights, internal deception, enmity against the Christian gospel."

On April 23, 1950, a message issued by the Church Administration of the Evangelical Church in Berlin-Brandenburg (of which Bishop Debelius was—and still is—the head) was read from the same pulpits. The basic challenge to the churches was described thus:

More than ever we see ourselves surrounded by harassed and restless consciences. Ceaselessly calls come from parishioners to the church administrations, to pastors and elders. They say, "Help us! We are being required to say something which, for the sake of the truth, we cannot say. We are being forced to participate in activities in which we cannot participate with a good conscience. We are supposed to approve of decisions which we cannot sanction. We are in constant danger of losing our freedom, employment and daily bread, if we decline to go along."

This need has everywhere become perceptibly sharpened by the heightened campaign for the National Front. Particularly shocking are the appeals of parents that their children are becoming more and more accustomed, under the pressure of schools, higher education and youth organizations, to speak and write differently than they think; that their Christian faith is despised, and that teachers try to talk them into believing that there is no God, and that Christ never existed.

Just before Stalin's death in 1953 there were seventy-two churchmen in prison serving sentences of from six months to twelve years (according to George Bailey in *The Reporter*, September 17, 1959). The charges in such cases are usually not for religious activities as such but for "activities inimical to the state," as had been the case earlier in the Soviet Union.

In recent years the most insidious device to undermine the church has been an elaborate communist ceremonial consecration of youth —*Jugendweihe*—which is intended to take the place of the church's confirmation. No youth who has not submitted to *Jugendweihe* is admitted to opportunities for higher education or to competition for any position under the control of the government. Thus parents and youth face agonizing and costly decisions.

The Churches and the Ideological Conflict

Whether in the Soviet Union, East Germany, or any other communist country, religious beliefs are attacked. Clear, thorough, persistent propaganda is supported by all the facilities, methods, and force available to the pervasive totalitarian regime. This is the basic theological conflict. It may be rather orderly. If the church contents itself with preparing the souls of believers for eternity through its rites and ceremonies and—aside from the theological issues—supports the communist program, it may not be seriously molested. If Christians as citizens keep their religious beliefs to themselves as private matters and do not let them interfere with public activities, they may have little trouble. When, on the other hand, churches and Christians as citizens oppose the social, political, and economic program, they face the drastic consequences of persecution.

It is therefore extremely dangerous to think of the conflict between free societies and communism primarily in the usual terms of power —military, economic, and political. To do so is to misunderstand the nature of the problem and to underestimate its seriousness.

Basically, the struggle is for the minds and wills of men. Wherever communism destroys the moral, intellectual, and spiritual integrity of men, freedom loses a battle. The first defense is religious. Behind that is the political line of defense; and, still farther back, the economic. The last desperate and probably futile line is the military; if we retreat to that or are driven to it because of our ineffectiveness on the primary fronts, the destruction will engulf us all. And yet our American public seems most concerned about the military position. It should not be neglected, but the public should also be concerned with the other lines as well.

Therefore, in our country as well as elsewhere, the churches' first task is to equip themselves for and to engage in the ideological encounter at the religious level. The communists are thoroughly indoctrinated and well trained. A Christian should not get into an argument with a communist in public or in private without at least an elementary course in theism. We do not face here the usual challenge that comes to our faith from other religions but the challenge of secularism that we find in mild and usually unaggressive forms in our own culture.

In its theory, communism is secularism reduced to its ultimate logic of dialectic materialism. Our theologically illiterate generation is not prepared to meet this challenge. Our young people should be given some basic training in theology so that they can explain—at least in an elementary way—*why* they believe in God, before being admitted to church membership.

Arguments about the technological and materialistic superiority of capitalism over communism—not so easily established as they were earlier—tend to confirm the basic philosophy of the communist that material achievement is the basis of everything desired by man.

Our case with regard to the value and dignity of man in relation to God and in society must be convincing. Freedom, honor, and ultimate truth—as distinguished from scientific facts—must be effectively asserted along with standards of living as goals of human existence. Standard of living must be put in its proper place as means, not the highest end. Only thus can we succeed in showing how communism degrades man.

But we must not oversimplify. The best statement of our case may be contradicted by our own conduct. Some of our magazines, movies, and television programs—especially advertising—give the impression that the American people are obsessed with material possessions as the chief end of life.

Our case must include the value of justice as well as freedom. At this point our racial discrimination is a devastating handicap in the ideological encounter.

Let us keep constantly in mind that the debate between theory and theory cannot be separated from a comparison of practice with practice. We get nowhere by comparing our principles with the bad features of communist practice. And we must point out the absurdity of comparing the idealism of communist theory with the worst features of our practice.

The Christian world view is an essential part of our ideological case. A religion of personal piety alone does not meet the universal and historical scope of the communist propaganda.

The Christian citizen should be the wisest, most courageous, most persistent, most cool-headed, and most effective antagonist of communism in the ideological struggle. The churches are such a crucial factor that they should not allow their policy to be determined for them by the exigencies of popular opinion but should act in accordance with their own faith, history, and function.

As a matter of policy they should include Christians "behind the curtains" in their world fellowship so long as they are bearing witness to Christian faith in the face of hostile atheism. The content and method of the witness of all within that fellowship are matters for discussion among themselves as well as by others.

They should challenge communism aggressively and confidently, but they should not encourage individuals to enter into direct encounter with it unless and until they are well prepared with an understanding of its ideology and of the theological reasoning with which to undermine it at its base.

They should be careful not to identify themselves with others simply on the ground that they are anti-communist. Some of the most glib talkers are morally disreputable in their personal conduct. The churches should not endorse them as allies and follow their lead in strategy, even though they may have been associated with a government group at some time.

Communism and Revolution

We should distinguish between communism and the revolutionary and undisciplined aspects of movements in other countries for self-determination. Such movements inevitably involve protest against the *status quo* and the powers that try to maintain it, including—sometimes—our own country. Communists invariably encourage violence and seek to infiltrate and gain control. But for us to characterize the movement as communist on those grounds in order to discredit it is wrong. It is unfair. It hurts anyone to be accused of communism when he is fighting it at first hand daily. Moreover, it gives credit to communists for victories they have not won and gives them prestige which contributes to their success where otherwise they might fail. Our general public judgments of certain disorders in Africa and Japan are cases in point.

The inevitability of change in the status of peoples, the fact that "change is not of itself evil," and the error of identifying peace with "perpetuation of the existing territorial and political order" were well defined in a statement on "Soviet-American Relations" submitted by the Commission on a Just and Durable Peace and adopted by the Executive Committee of the Federal Council of Churches on October 11, 1946. That statement is still useful for policy guidance, though the international situation has changed.

This chapter on communism has been placed toward the end of the book, because the mandate for the involvement of the churches in public affairs is essential to it. Without some such mandate, they would be justified in withdrawing from the contest with communism except to minister to the faithful who come to them, to conduct worship for them, and to "prepare their souls for eternity." We cannot deny the responsibility of our own churches with regard to public affairs and at the same time insist upon such responsibility for churches in communist countries. They and we are of the same "Holy Catholic Church" of the creed, under the same God, and accountable to the same Judge.

The Local and National Levels

In considering the action of the churches in the field of public affairs, there is no more futile discussion than the attempt to distinguish between the local church, the denomination, the local and state councils of churches, the National Council of Churches, and the World Council of Churches in terms of their relative importance. They are all essential. They are all interdependent. There is no point in trying to establish a scale of rating of their respective values or strategic advantage.

Votes in the United Nations or in Washington are important. But in the long run they are determined by the desires expressed and the conclusions reached in local communities as indicated by their votes for congressmen, senators, and presidents, and by the opinions communicated to those they have elected. United Nations votes are in large measure determined by instructions from national governments.

Representatives sooner or later are either supported or repudiated by their people. In our form of government the control is direct and immediate. Even in totalitarian nations the will of the people ultimately makes a difference.

As in the governmental realm, so also in the churches. The World Council of Churches is controlled by its 172 member national denominational bodies. The denominations are in turn controlled by their local churches, except in some totalitarian nations where the national denominational bodies are under coercion by the national government. In our country the National Council of Churches is controlled by its national denominational members.

It would seem, then, that the local churches are the most basic factor. In terms of ultimate decision, they are. But the situation is complicated and qualified by the nature of modern society. The information and assumptions on the basis of which the people in the local church make their decisions are influenced—in some instances controlled—by power structures which manipulate many of the mass media of communication and the propaganda organizations at the national level. Local groups are therefore not as independent as they sometimes assume.

National church agencies, denominational and interdenominational, and the World Council of Churches are in a better position than local churches to know about interests and purposes that condition the national newspaper, magazine, radio, television, and other impacts upon the people. It is a function of the world and national organizations to deal with these interests.

People who work at the local level should not envy or feel inferior to those who work at the centers of national power and decision. There is an element of obvious drama in testifying before congressional committees and interviewing delegates to the United Nations. The scenes of such activities are impressive, and the people involved are in conspicuous positions of leadership and in the news. But the obvious and dramatic are not always the significant.

Representatives of the churches are not taken seriously very long in governmental or intergovernmental circles unless the views they express are demonstratively those of the churches. And the attitudes and convictions of the churches are developed primarily in the local congregations. These in turn are influenced, more or less, by the facts and insights provided to them by their national agencies. Thus national and local are interdependent.

When national church agency leaders deal with the national centers of power which mold public opinion, they are confronted not only with considerations of what is good or bad, but also with what the people want and will pay for. Consumer tastes and demands are developed by local as well as national influences. The form and content of movies, radio and television programs, and the magazines with circulations in the millions are determined in large measure by what the people want to read, see, and hear. What is popular is good business. We who deal with the national officials are usually told that the mass media are business enterprises, not reform agencies, and that if the churches do not approve of their products it is up to the churches to change the public taste and demand. This is not to say that there are no leaders in the mass media who have a sense of public responsibility. There are. And they are justified in asking our support when we approve their policies, programs, and publications. We should write them about it, buy tickets, and subscribe. Here again the support and influence provided are by individuals and from the local community.

The National Council of Churches maintains an office in Washington. It is not a lobby. Its function is rather to inform the churches on

what is going on in the national capital so that they may know what
policies are in the process of being formulated and where and when
to express their opinions if they have a concern. They are not told
what opinion to express. An alert, responsible, and informed constituency at the "grass roots" is more important and in the long run
more effective than a lobby in Washington. Without it, a church lobby
would be irresponsible and futile, even if it were sound in principle,
which is very doubtful. And a lobby is not necessary to obtain a hear-
ing. Abundant opportunity is provided, usually by invitation, for representatives of church agencies to testify before congressional committees and to share their information and advice with executive officers.

After thirty-five years of experience in local churches and in city,
state, national, and world councils of churches, and extensive dealing
with governmental procedures in Washington, I find it impossible to
judge one level of operation—local, national, or world—more important strategically than the others.

Fortunately the attempt to distinguish is irrelevant. Most of us who
are in churches related to the councils share in one orderly, co-ordinated fellowship having local, regional, national, and world denominational and interdenominational bodies which together enable us to
bear effective witness. The fact that there is no central controlling
authority in this pattern of relationships accentuates the responsibility
of the several denominations and their local churches. Decentralized
initiative and responsibility, voluntarily co-ordinated, are the key to
effective action by the churches in public affairs.

CHAPTER VI

Ten Urgent Emphases

We have analyzed the responsibility of the churches in public affairs and reviewed their policy and action in the major social-problem areas. With all this in mind, we now should try to identify and select the most urgent needs of man in his present condition in the social scene in which he lives and works in this country—the world of public affairs.

In my judgment his greatest need is for a better understanding of himself and for some guiding principles or insights that will give him a confident sense of direction in his social experience and decisions.

The primary role of the churches is always the proclamation of the timeless, unchanging Gospel and the mediation of God's grace. Man's basic needs are unchanging, but the context in which they are experienced is new every day. The churches' special responsibility and contribution in relation to public affairs is therefore to interpret the truth of the Gospel in such a way as to make it obviously relevant to man's needs today.

I suggest, therefore, that in service to God, to our nation, and to people, churches and Christian citizens should:

1. *Reassert the importance of the individual person.*

Groups obviously count today. We organize to get things done. "Organization man" occasionally comes to self-consciousness out of the nightmare of frenzied activity and asks who he is and whether he is slave or free.

Machines count—literally as well as figuratively. Is a man working with a machine its attendant or its master?

Nature is beautiful, and lavish—in our country—as it rewards man's labor to satisfy his physical needs; but it is also ruthless and no respecter of persons when it unleashes a hurricane.

The modern city can be cruelly indifferent to an individual. There is no place where one can be more lonely than in a crowd. He can lose himself in a crowd but seldom find himself.

The depersonalizing aspects of modern society, man's "lostness," and the cheapness of life in a technological age call for a reaffirmation of the individual's worth, not alone but in community. They call for a fresh study of the Bible from the Genesis story of the creation, through the Psalms and Prophets to the parables and deeds of Jesus. They also indicate that the church especially must make the individual aware of his value to God and to other people. The church cares about him as a whole person; others regard him as a body, a mind, a voter, a producer, a consumer, or a passenger.

2. *Interpret the meaning of life.*

There are plenty of authorities to interpret the meaning of this or that aspect of life, but the Gospel is our final authority on the meaning of life itself. If life were only a biological phenomenon, then political and economic affairs could be guided by the ethics of the struggle for survival. But life is much more than that.

Psychology and the social sciences can help people with problems of adjustment, but adjustment is no substitute for an understanding of what we are. Only when we know what we are can we decide what we want and what we do not want in public affairs. Hitler had one understanding of the meaning of life. As people yielded to it, public affairs in Germany became conformed to it. The Marxist communist has another understanding; the King of Saudi Arabia, another; and the Founding Fathers of our country, still another. Each is based on elemental beliefs.

Our generation can recite a few phrases from the Declaration of Independence, but can it define the philosophy of which it is an expression? We have inherited certain forms and processes of political, economic, and social life to which we are committed as a matter of tradition and because they have worked well for us. But our ethical standards have become increasingly subject to determination by pragmatic expediency rather than by principle.

It is high time for us to articulate quite definitely the beliefs and principles that guide us in our conduct and determine what we expect in public affairs. We are in the dangerous position of improvising public decisions, largely on the basis of compromise between conflicting interests. Our decisions should derive from principles which we hold firmly, from our understanding of the meaning of life.

This is predominently a task for churches and Christian citizens.

3. *Clarify the nature of freedom.*

Too many of our people think of freedom in terms of the absence of laws and other restraints in political, economic, and social affairs. They want to do what they want to do without hindrance, and they often discover that they do not know what they want. They need to understand the necessity of surrender to a great purpose or commitment to an absorbing loyalty or cause. They must see the difference between liberty and license.

Our people need to understand that political and economic freedom, though highly important, do not in and of themselves give a person the release his spirit seeks. One may escape from the slavery of drudgery, only to enter the enervating bondage of an endless round of bridge clubs, cocktail parties, and the frenzied pursuit of trivial amusement.

4. *Examine the significance of a "standard of living."*

What is the difference between one's standard of living and his happiness—his helpfulness as a neighbor? Is it true, as advertising implies, that the more we have, the happier we are? How high a minimum standard of living is society morally obligated to guarantee? How is the "highest standard of living," which is claimed by our nation, to be defined? Justice still requires concern for the living standards of people in poverty. But how many other people are warping their lives in the frantic pursuit of things they do not need?

Our concern for a higher standard of living for people in our own country and other countries who are below the level of health and decency is quite another matter.

This is a question of the utmost importance in our ideological competition with communism. Until we clarify our standards of value in this respect we shall also leave our friends in other countries perplexed as to what Americans live for.

5. *Develop ethical standards for power groups.*

The ethical standards of interpersonal relationships are not adequate to guide people in many of their quandaries with regard to organizational relationships in the power structure of mass society. What is the individual Christian citizen's responsibility for the actions of a special-interest group of which he is a member?

Many a Christian will support a trade association, labor union, medical association, or farmers' organization in doing things he would never think of doing himself. And officers or agents of such groups are often expected to act in a representative capacity in ways which they would repudiate for themselves personally.

Somehow we assume that selfish interest served by a group is under less ethical restraint than in the case of an individual. And yet the group is composed of individuals.

With policies and contracts increasingly determined by groups rather than by individuals, Christian citizens have a responsibility to examine the conduct of power groups.

6. *Warn the nation of the moral hazards of its power.*

Would that we had a Kipling to write a "Recessional" for the United States today! The one he wrote has sufficient relevance for us today to merit interpretation. As a nation we are off guard to temptation because the power we build is not an end in itself but a requirement for defense of the free world. Nevertheless, it is power, and power is morally hazardous.

The life of the rich uncle is never easy, and "the policeman's lot is not a happy one." The United States is cast in both roles with little experience in either. We resent not being appreciated. We tend to be sensitive and defensive. In such a situation there is danger that we become unaware of the moral temptations of power and wealth.

7. *Define worthy objectives for the nation.*

As a nation we have come dangerously close to allowing the challenge of communism to determine our objectives as a people. We are more preoccupied with defense than with adventure. There is no question that we have been required to face a serious menace. But we are trying so hard to outdo communism in scientific achievement and technological power that we are in danger of becoming a technological society, to the neglect of our traditional purpose of developing a quality of manhood and a way of life that would appeal to all mankind as the most important goal for human striving.

Moreover, our present position is not conducive to the critical self-appraisal that is so essential to the health and growth of a democratic society. When every admission of a fault or an abuse is exploited by communist propaganda as if it were a chief characteristic of our nation, self-criticism seems to weaken our position in the world. Consequently it is especially urgent now that we define new goals of justice, freedom, and brotherhood toward which to strive, lest we stagnate in defensiveness of what we have already achieved. Let us not permit others to chart the areas and limits of our national program and aspiration.

8. *Declare the sovereignty of God.*

Modern man has become so accustomed to the amazing achievements of science and the appalling power of nuclear energy that his fate appears to him, superficially, to rest with physical factors; and history seems to be a blind struggle in the dark. Today, especially, the sovereignty of God must be reiterated constantly and defined carefully.

This belief is essential to an understanding of the appropriate role of the nation. It is also the basis for a rational philosophy of history, for without it history makes no sense except under some such assumption as Marxist dialectic materialism. The choice is before us. We dare not be indifferent.

The sovereignty of God is also the corrective to man's pride as well as to his despair, in private thought and in relation to social problems. It is, finally, the ground of our hope.

9. *Realize the corporate fellowship of the church.*

This is especially needed today in view of the increased mobility of our population, the rootlessness of many people, the loneliness of depersonalized urban life, for it draws the individual out of isolation into belonging to the most meaningful community. I am not raising here the whole theological question of the nature of the church, but only calling attention to a need of man accentuated by contemporary society.

In the face of conflicts between nations, the wider corporate fellowship of the church helps to hold the world together. In the nation it maintains a sense of community where there are tensions in economic life. It bridges all the separations between the races. It is the most healing factor in much social welfare service.

It is in being actually, inherent in the nature of the church, and yet it has to be acknowledged and cultivated. Some churches deny it by their attitudes and practices. It is relevant to public affairs at every point.

10. *Witness to the principle of redemption.*

Our world in all its affairs desperately needs an understanding of the cross, not only as an event in history, but also as a revelation of what is essential in history.

Christ's death for our salvation is crucial. But He Himself said, "If any man would come after me, let him deny himself and take up his cross daily and follow me" (Luke 9:23). We do not presume to do what He did. But He revealed God's way in human life and history.

The redemptive principle, manifested in acts and testimony, is essential in Christian discipleship. Without it, love is not complete Christian love.

St. Paul said that when he preached Christ crucified it was "a stumbling-block to Jews and folly to Gentiles" (I Cor. 1:23). They were not evil people; they had an incorrect understanding of God's way with man. Who are those who in our day hold the same assumptions as "the Jews" and "the Gentiles" of His day? I do not judge. But I am convinced that contemporary society has a tragic and perhaps fateful blind spot with regard to the principle or doctrine of redemption. It assumes that human wisdom, ingenuity, and more education are enough to solve human social problems. They are essential, because man must use all his resources in the service of God and his neighbor. But there is a deeper cost for challenging human sin and conflict.

I do not presume to give an adequate definition of the principle of redemption, but for me it includes the voluntary giving of self and the yielding of self-advantage out of concern and compassion for the sin and suffering of others.

If Christ revealed God's way of dealing with weak and sinful, estranged and lost man—and I believe He did—then to contemplate Him upon the cross is to understand God's purpose and the way of dealing with evil among men. It is to find the key to the Gospel, the churches, public affairs, history, and man's destiny. For after the cross came the resurrection.

I believe the depth of insight and the value perspective to be derived from attention to such points as these ten would enable the churches and Christians to add more significantly to the approach to public affairs than merely to cultivate "Christian motivation" and write theological footnotes to popular analyses.

These are fateful days for our nation and for our people. They are days of challenging opportunities for the churches. They are great days in which to be living for those who see God at work in the world and know that He guides and supports those who trust in Him. May He help us.